Control and Coordination of Subsidiaries in Japanese Corporate Groups

Control and Coordination of Subsidiaries in Japanese Corporate Groups

Akira Mitsumasu
Japan Airlines Co., Ltd.

World Scientific

NEW JERSEY • LONDON • SINGAPORE • BEIJING • SHANGHAI • HONG KONG • TAIPEI • CHENNAI

Published by

World Scientific Publishing Co. Pte. Ltd.
5 Toh Tuck Link, Singapore 596224
USA office: 27 Warren Street, Suite 401-402, Hackensack, NJ 07601
UK office: 57 Shelton Street, Covent Garden, London WC2H 9HE

British Library Cataloguing-in-Publication Data
A catalogue record for this book is available from the British Library.

**CONTROL AND COORDINATION OF SUBSIDIARIES IN JAPANESE
CORPORATE GROUPS**

ISBN 978-981-4675-70-3

In-house Editor: Sandhya Venkatesh

Typeset by Stallion Press
Email: enquiries@stallionpress.com

Printed in Singapore

PREFACE

This book is written for thoughtful managers and executives, academics interested in the intersection of management theory and practice, and students who are interested in management and strategy. It will be of interest both to readers with an interest in Japanese business, and to those with an interest in effective management of corporate groups.

Over the years, many books and articles have been written about Japanese business groups, or *keiretsu*. Though these collections of independent companies, linked through minority ownership stakes and close exchange, were an important factor behind Japan's rapid economic development, the *keiretsu* and their importance have declined, as Japan has become a mature economy. Instead, corporate groups, consisting of parent companies and their closely related subsidiaries, have increased in size and importance. In the last decades, many Japanese companies have significantly increased the size of their corporate groups; at the same time they have decreased the size and scope of their core company.

Despite their importance, very little has been written on corporate groups in Japan, and this book is a very important step towards filling the gap in our knowledge — both empirical and theoretical. This book bridges theory and practice, providing a very extensive analysis of business groups both from theoretical and practical perspectives. It combines a deep theoretical perspective with detailed analysis of the actual state of corporate groups in Japan, and by doing so, has lessons for both practitioners and academics. This book's objective, to expand practitioners' understanding of the academic theory around corporate groups, as well as to enlighten academics on the actual state of Japanese corporate groups, is achieved very successfully.

This book gives us some very valuable glimpses into how several prominent Japanese companies manage their corporate groups, and suggests that companies make considerable effort into coordination and monitoring of their groups, but tend to lack a systematic way to categorize group firms, identify their function, and relate management and control practices to desired outcomes. In other words, firms often do not have much of a strategy for managing their large and growing corporate groups. The book provides a useful framework to help managers take their first steps towards a group strategy — requiring them first to identify the type and function of the group firm. The case studies provide reveal how leading Japanese companies manage their groups.

Chapters 2 and 3 of this volume provide an overview of the evolution of the Japanese corporate system and Japanese corporate groups. Chapter 4 is an in depth discussion of theory by both Japanese and international scholars on corporate groups. The discussion of theory is continued in Chapter 5, with a deeper exposition on issues such as monitoring, power, control and incentives in the parent–subsidiary relationship. Chapter 6 bridges theory and practice with case studies of five corporate groups: Hitachi, Panasonic, Mitsubishi Heavy Industries, Nihon Yusen and Japan Airlines. Chapter 7 offers original analysis and a framework for classifying subsidiaries, identifying possible management problems, and creating more successful subsidiaries.

One of the most important and unusual aspects of this book is that it shows very clearly where academic literature and practical wisdom overlap, and how they go in very different directions when it comes to Japanese corporate groups. We learn that Japanese companies manage their group firms based on experience, intuition, and often, try either to apply a "one size fits all" policy to a very diverse group of subsidiaries, or address subsidiary issues in an *ad hoc* fashion. As corporate groups grow in importance for Japanese firms, managers would do well to think more carefully about the role of each subsidiary.

While this book is about Japanese firms, its findings have implications for corporate groups in other countries. Making careful and deliberate decisions about the role of each subsidiary, looking at the relationship from the subsidiary and parent's perspectives, understanding the nature of unilateral or mutual dependence and its implications are all important tasks for managers in any firm that has a corporate group. This book will also be very useful to Japanese business scholars as it draws attention to an important new trend in Japanese business, and provides much-needed insights on ongoing changes in the Japanese company. There is a great wealth of information and insight here, and I strongly believe that this book will provide both guidance and insight to business practitioners, as well as stimulate new research into Japanese corporate groups.

Christina L. Ahmadjian
Hitotsubashi University

CONTENTS

Chapter 1

INTRODUCTION

Most newspaper and business magazine articles on strategic moves of large corporations, tend to mention that corporations have full control over their activities, enabling them to invest in new businesses or refocusing on core ones. Given that there are hundreds of subsidiaries of large Japanese corporations, and a daunting task of coordinating masses of activities across organizations, one begins to wonder just how much control there really is? How do companies manage their subsidiaries? And more fundamentally, why do many large Japanese companies choose to pursue such a strategy?

Kikkawa (2007) and Shimotani (1993), for example, suggested that firms choose to have subsidiaries so as to sub-divide managerial responsibilities into smaller units, and in doing so, attain clearer accountability as well as quicker decision-making. This may be true for some cases, but from my conversations with many practitioners, it appears that many companies cannot explain well why they choose to pursue a group strategy, and why their current parent–subsidiary relationships stand where they are. There appears also to be only very few existing literatures on the subject of corporate groups. Ito, Kikutani and Hayashida (2008) described that "theoretical or empirical study of business group in our sense is scarce, in contrast to a large body of literature on other types of business groups." Similarly, Johnston (2005) noted that "the headquarter–subsidiary link still remains a black box." One reason as to why relatively little attention has been paid to subsidiaries may be because they have been regarded by many academics, especially in the U.S., to be not significantly different from business divisions, and hence do not need to be dealt with separately (Ito and Shishido, 2001).

But if we see subsidiaries as a substantial part of what makes up a corporate group, its routines and its core competencies, then the control and coordination of subsidiaries becomes a crucial management issue that merits more attention. It is also an increasingly relevant issue in Japan today where, as pointed out by Miyajima (2011), we witness many Japanese corporations are establishing or expanding subsidiaries, such that information asymmetries between the corporate head-office and the many layers of internal organizations and subsidiaries have become much greater.

One primary objective of this book is to bridge academic knowledge and practitioner's knowledge regarding the control and coordination of subsidiaries, whilst providing also related materials that hopefully would help readers who are not familiar with Japanese corporate groups to have an overview of some of their characteristics. Two fundamental questions in particular will be explored. The first question is why do corporations establish subsidiaries and form corporate groups? And the second is how do corporate groups manage their subsidiaries?

In trying to answer these two questions, I conducted a series of interviews with five large Japanese corporate groups between September 2012 and January 2013, and collected archival data as well as IR and news sources that were available, so as to observe real life situations and compare them with related academic knowledge. I also held discussions with nine other corporate groups between June and September 2013 through four sessions of group study that were organised by the Business Research Institute in Tokyo. Through these discussions, I was able to verify some of the initial findings that I have made in my earlier interviews.

With regards to academic theories, the materials that I have chosen for the purpose of this book are neither exhaustive nor necessarily specific to the issue of corporate group management. However, I do hope that by utilising some of these major theories and mapping them against group management practices, the end result would shed some light on corporate group management practices in Japan.

This book is organized as follows. Chapter 2 gives a definition of corporate group in Japan and distinguishes it from the *keiretsu* business group, which is a term used to describe groups of independent corporations that cluster, have cross ownership and collaborate under their flagship main bank that provides finance to its member corporations. Chapter 3 provides a backdrop and context for understanding the corporate landscape in which Japanese firms today operate. The chapter also describes how Japanese corporations, faced with challenges on many fronts in an increasingly globalized and modularized world where the Japan model is said to have little comparative advantage, have been adapting to changes.

Chapters 4 and 5 provide a literature review on some of the major literatures that are related to the research questions concerning why corporate groups exist and how they are managed. Chapter 6 attempts to bridge academic knowledge with practitioners knowledge by looking at five corporate groups: Hitachi, Panasonic, Mitsubishi Heavy Industry, Nihon Yusen and Japan Airlines, and by identifying areas where practitioner's knowledge could be used to expand existing theories. Chapter 6 also looks at the control systems that Japanese corporate groups use for coordinating planning, executing strategy, and optimizing overall group performance.

The case study also identifies "dependency" as a crucial factor that affects parent–subsidiary relationships. In Chapter 7, based on this dependency relationship, a four-part classification of subsidiaries is proposed to facilitate the discussion of different issues that arise under different parent–subsidiary settings. By combining academic and practitioner's knowledge, Chapter 8 attempts to illustrate a simplistic roadmap for creating successful subsidiary management. Chapter 9 concludes this book with a brief summary of major findings and their contribution to the knowledge of corporate group management, and discusses areas for future research.

Chapter 2

CORPORATE GROUPS
IN JAPAN

2.1 DEFINITION OF A CORPORATE GROUP
IN JAPAN

In order to be clear about what I mean by a corporate group, I begin by drawing a distinction with a much wider topic — that of "business groups" in general. The terms "corporate group" and "business group" or "*keiretsu*" as I will explain, are not synonymous. A business group is defined as "firms which though legally independent, are bound together by a constellation of formal and informal ties and are accustomed to taking coordinated action" (Khanna and Rivkin, 2001), and as "an intermediate case of organization structure between market contracting and a common-ownership integration of multiple production units called a conglomerate" (Khanna and Yafeh, 2005). These definitions of a business group are somewhat arbitrary, and may be used to mean anything from the Korean *chaebols* to loose coalitions of firms in which no single firm holds controlling interests in the other firms. In the concluding remarks of a meta-analysis on business group affiliation, Carney *et al.* (2010) commented that "business groups come in many shapes and sizes and their heterogeneity across time and place defies any simple explanation."

With such heterogeneity, there is thus a wide range of literature concerning business groups, many of which try to explain the benefits and costs of group affiliation. For example, Granovetter (1995) quoted four often given reasons for group affiliation, namely (a) firms are rarely self-sufficient and will need to form connections with other firms upon whom they depend for resources, (b) firms need to form strategic alliances to cope with changing market environment, (c) collusion purposes, (d) firms' desire to extract rents through coalition. Claessens, Fan and Lang (2002) on the other hand studied the benefits and costs of group affiliation in East Asia by looking at how agency problems affect firm value. While Samphantharak (2007) used costs of ownership and costs of market contracting to explain the existence of business groups, and highlighted the flexibility in ownership compositions as their advantages. Other reasons that explain group formation include market failure and institutional voids such as limitations in a society's financial, legal, and labour market institutions (Leff, 1978), and benefits of market power by horizontal integration and collusion (Bernheim and Whinston, 1990).

In the business group literature concerning Japanese corporations, much focus has been on the Japanese *keiretsu*, and factors that motivate and glue individual companies to form business groups. Khanna and Yafeh (2005), for example, in discussing the role of business groups, mentioned in their work that the *keiretsu* offers a form of mutual risk sharing where the group's main bank intervenes to assist distressed member firms. They, however, concluded that this popular view of risk sharing is not evident elsewhere, where other reasons are more likely to explain the ubiquity of business groups around the world.

In Japan, the six large financial *keiretsus* are Mitsubishi, Sumitomo, Mitsui, Fuyo, Sanwa and Ichikan. Within a *keiretsu* group is usually a main bank and a large conglomerate trading company that coordinate and foster transactions within the group. Member firms within the *keiretsu* display a high degree of institutional isomorphism, and reflect a rather homogeneous national model with relative low variation across firms relative to more liberal market economies. Over the past decades however, with the restructuring of Japanese corporations in the post bubble period of the 1990s, and active cross boundary collaborations and consolidation of banks into mega banks, the boundary of these financial *keiretsus* have become increasingly vague. Financial dependence and intra-*keiretsu* procurement have declined, and many member companies now participate in multiple *keiretsu* presidents' councils, which are essentially cross share-holder meetings.

This is not to say that the study of *keiretsu* or business group formations in Japan has become less relevant. Indeed, large Japanese companies still have large networks of relational contracts and the strategy of leveraging capabilities within business groups is still very much an important and relevant topic today. But in comparison to the much researched *keiretsu*, there seems to be a proportionately small number of studies on Japanese corporate groups, a topic which has grown in importance since the revision of Securities and Exchange Act in 2000, which made mandatory the disclosure of corporate groups' consolidated financial statements. As a result of this Act, companies became more conscious of their consolidated financial performance, of corporate social responsibilities as a group, and of the board of directors' legal responsibilities in maintaining appropriate control over activities of their subsidiaries and related companies within the corporate group.

The study of corporate groups in Japan can perhaps be seen as a subset of the wider context of business groups. There are many areas in common such as the Coasian question of why do firms or business groups exist? Or on relational contracts, which focus on how self-enforceable terms can be supported without the use of enforceable contract because repeated interaction within a well-defined group such as a business or corporate group with a set of shared norms governing the behaviour of group members leads to cooperation and implicit self-enforcing obligations. But despite many commonalities, there are notable differences. For example, the issue of linkage motivation such as kinship, ethnic background and trust among component firms would be a more relevant topic in the study of business groups than in the study of corporate groups, where financial origins and control rights often mandate solidarity.

Having made a distinction between a business group and a corporate group, let us now look at some formal definitions of Corporate Groups in Japan. According to Article 2-1-26 of Securities Listing

Regulations in Japan, a Corporate Group is defined as a corporation together with its subsidiaries and related companies. A similar definition is given in Article 4-1-1 of Regulation concerning Consolidated Financial Statements (also Cabinet Ordinance No. 45 of 30th September 2010), which states that a Corporate Group is the Corporate and its subsidiaries that submit a Consolidated Financial Statement. A subsidiary is defined under Article 2-3 of Company Law as a company whose majority voting rights are being held by another company, and whose management is also controlled by that company. Article 3-1 of Order for Enforcement of the Companies Act adds that a subsidiary is such when the decisions of its financial and business policies are being controlled by another company.

There is a distinction between a subsidiary company, which is controlled by its parent company, and a related company which is influenced by its parent company. In other words, the degree of control and influence determines whether an affiliated company is a subsidiary or whether it is a related company. Figure 1 illustrates this distinction. The figure also shows that a corporate group consists of consolidated subsidiaries and related companies as well as non-consolidated subsidiaries and related companies, with the latter having negligible impact on the corporate group's performance.

The above definition is the result of financial reporting requirements aimed at increasing the transparency of Japanese corporations. For the period ending 31st March 2000, publicly listed firms were required, for the first time, to provide consolidated financial statements that included results from subsidiaries and related companies over which they had *de facto* control or substantial influence. Although a corporate group consists of both subsidiary and related companies, the focus of this book concerns subsidiary companies only. There are two reasons for choosing to do so. Firstly, my interest is on the intriguing characteristic of parent and subsidiary relationship which may range from a high degree of control by the parent over its subsidiary, to a more arm's length market transaction like relationship. As for related companies, because ownership is only partial, it is not easy for the parent to exert direct control, unless there are pre-agreed contractual terms that allow control over specific

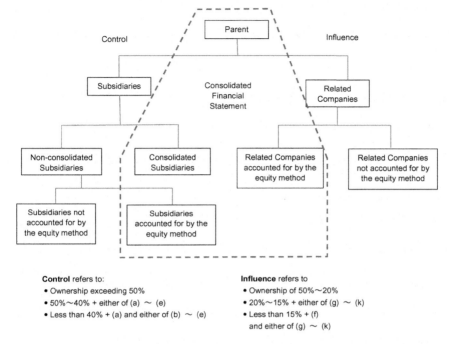

Control refers to:
- Ownership exceeding 50%
- 50%~40% + either of (a) ~ (e)
- Less than 40% + (a) and either of (b) ~ (e)

Influence refers to
- Ownership of 50%~20%
- 20%~15% + either of (g) ~ (k)
- Less than 15% + (f) and either of (g) ~ (k)

Figure 1: Corporate group

(a) Together with persons of close relationship and persons in agreement (e.g. people who would exercise voting rights in agreement on issues such as investment, technology, transaction, HR and wages), the sum of voting rights exceeds 50%.

(b) Executive directors or persons capable of exerting influence over important financial and strategic decisions, have majority control over the board of directors or equivalent function.

(c) There exists contracts that enable control over important financial and strategic decisions.

(d) Provider of over 50% of total finance or collaterals.

(e) Where there exists evidence of control by other decision making institutions.

(f) Together with persons of close relationship and persons in agreement, the sum of voting rights exceeds 20%.

(g) Where the parent's executive director or others assume important roles in the subsidiary such as CEO or board member.

(h) Provider(s) of important finance or collaterals.

(i) Provider(s) of important technology.

(j) Important client or transaction partner.

(k) Where there exists evidence of substantial influence over financial and business decisions.

areas. Secondly, the diversity of related companies, which may range from an important manufacturing sub-contractor to an interest-based relationship, such as for the sake of having a stake and a voice in an entity for industry political reasons, makes generalization difficult and increases complexity without necessarily adding value to the focus of this research.

2.2 A BRIEF OVERVIEW OF CORPORATE GROUPS IN JAPAN

With the term "corporate group" defined in the previous section, this section gives a brief overview of corporate groups in Japan. Based on the 2009 Economic Census published by the Ministry of Internal Affairs and Communications in December 2011, there are 26,701 corporate groups in Japan, with a total of 63,163 subsidiary companies. Tables 1, 2 and 3 taken from the census data show the number of corporate group and their subsidiaries by firm size measured by capital, the number of subsidiaries per corporate group and the number of employees respectively.

It can be observed that many corporate groups have just a few subsidiaries. But there are very large corporate groups such as Sony which has 1,277 subsidiaries, Hitachi has 913, Orix 784, NTT 756, Nihon Yusen 687, Panasonic 633, Sumitomo Trading 578,

Table 1:   Number of corporate groups by firm size

Size of Parent Company by Capital	Number of Corporate Groups	Number of Subsidiary Companies
Less than 3 million yen	127	159
3~5 million yen	1,114	1,210
5~10 million yen	597	657
10~30 million yen	9,570	11,694
30~50 million yen	4,366	6,010
50~100 million yen	4,646	7,854
100~300 million yen	2,199	4,723
300~1 billion yen	1,510	4,523
1~5 billion yen	1,293	5,782
More than 5 billion yen	1,251	20,516
Total	26,701	63,163

Table 2: Number of subsidiaries within corporate groups

Number of Subsidiaries within Group	Number of Corporate Groups	Percentage
1	18,742	70.2
2	3,725	14.0
3	1,530	5.7
4	707	2.6
5~9	1,207	4.5
10~19	458	1.7
20~29	132	0.5
30~49	104	0.4
More than 50	96	0.4
Total	26,701	100.0

Fujitsu 555, Toyota 511 and Toshiba 498. (Note: These numbers are taken from the respective companies' 2010 financial reports). Figure 2 shows the distribution of the number of subsidiaries for 3,037 listed parent companies in the Tokyo Stock Exchange, while Figure 3 shows the average number of subsidiary companies in the First Division over a period of fifteen years.

If we look only at the Tokyo Stock Exchange's first section, the average number of consolidated subsidiaries has nearly doubled from 18 in 1990 to 34 in 2000. This rise since has been moderate with an average of 36 subsidiaries in 2005. The average of the largest 200 firms has risen more substantially from around 45 in 1990 to 108 in 2005.

According to the annual Basic Survey of Corporate Activities (*Kigyou Katsudo Kihon Chousa*) conducted by the Ministry of Economy, Trade and Industry (METI) as of 31st March 2012, 12,361 firms (43.6%) out of the 29,570 firms from which data were collected, have subsidiary or related companies. Table 4 shows the breakdown by industry. The total number of their affiliated companies amounts to 85,352, out of which 51,312 (60%) are inside Japan, and 34,040 (40%) are outside Japan.

The manufacturing sector has the largest number of affiliated companies, and the proportion of overseas affiliated companies has been on the rise over the past two decades, as more and more manufacturing companies shift their production overseas. These statistics

Table 3: Number of employees within corporate groups

Number of Full Time Employee in Parent Company	Number of Corporate Groups	Number of Subsidiary Companies	Number of Offices	Total Number of Employees	Paid Executives	Full Time Employees	Temporary Employees
0~9	2,551	5,220	5,642	25,452	9,936	12,785	2,731
10~19	2,745	5,708	6,955	55,416	11,949	39,445	4,022
20~29	2,267	4,849	6,608	70,650	11,161	55,023	4,466
30~49	3,400	7,471	12,084	158,930	18,674	132,125	8,131
50~99	4,598	10,598	22,351	375,390	29,807	329,005	16,578
100~299	5,801	15,304	51,045	1,096,022	50,368	1,005,639	40,015
300~999	3,272	12,378	73,764	1,864,545	44,219	1,737,997	82,329
1,000~1,999	896	5,479	47,792	1,331,254	20,594	1,260,338	50,322
2,000~4,999	638	6,227	70,554	2,122,181	22,438	1,962,770	136,973
5,000~9,999	262	4,584	51,975	1,933,530	15,819	1,836,511	81,200
10,000~19,999	135	3,848	56,116	1,949,651	14,794	1,861,829	73,028
20,000~49,999	96	4,597	68,747	2,916,523	16,956	2,808,942	90,625
More than 50,000	40	3,601	104,133	4,519,027	15,665	4,374,752	128,610
Total	26,701	89,864	577,756	18,418,571	282,380	17,417,161	719,030

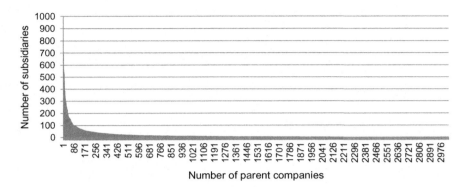

Figure 2:   Number of subsidiary companies

Note: Data obtained in February 2011.

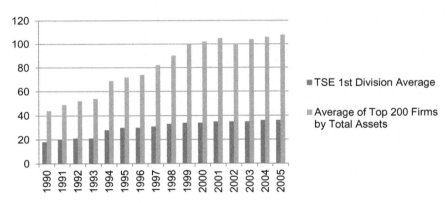

Figure 3:   Average number of subsidiary companies

Source: Miyajima (2011) p. 257, Figs. 6.3.

show that more and more Japanese companies are pursuing group formation or expansion as their strategy.

With regards to the relationship between the consolidated group and its affiliated companies, investment on and finance provided to affiliated companies constitute nearly 70% of total investment and assets, whilst transactions with affiliated companies amount to 20.3% (33.7% in manufacturing) of total revenue, and 24.6% (33.0% in manufacturing) of total procurement. Payments to affiliated companies for technology amount to 23% of total technology payments to all

Table 4: Number of companies that have affiliated companies

	2008	2009	2010	2011
Total	11,753	11,816	12,050	12,361
Manufacturing	5,890	5,903	5,943	5,986
Electricity and Gas	84	84	80	87
Information and Telecommunication	785	833	870	886
Wholesale	2,831	2,815	2,850	2,985
Retail	1,211	1,199	1,250	1,255
Others	952	982	1,057	1,162

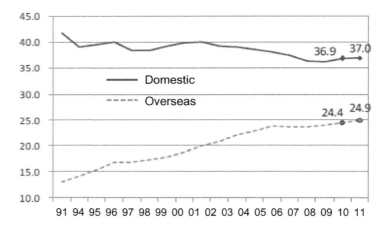

Figure 4: Percentage of manufacturing firms that have affiliated companies

companies, whilst revenue from affiliated companies for technology makes up 51% of total technology revenue from all companies. These figures show that there is a certain amount of interdependency between the affiliated companies and the consolidated business group.

Concerning group formation, subsidiaries may be hived off from a corporate function or business division, established as a new venture, or acquired through M&A. The number of IN–OUT M&A,[1]

---

[1] In–Out M&A denotes Japanese company's acquisition of foreign company. Out–In M&A denotes foreign company's acquisition of Japanese company. In–In M&A denotes Japanese company's acquisition of Japanese company.

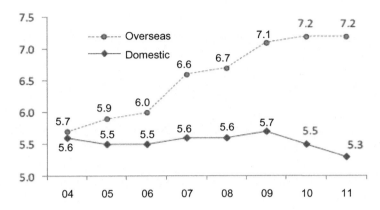

Figure 5:　Number of affiliated companies per manufacturing firm

which were active in the bubble period of the 1980s diminished in the post bubble years or choose and focus, and we witnessed instead a surge in In–In M&A as shown in the Figure 6 below.

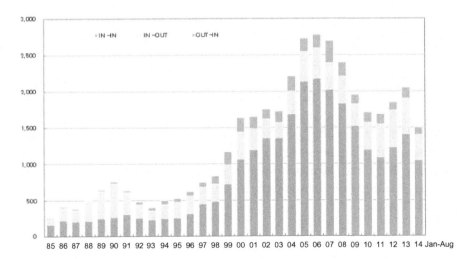

Figure 6:　M&A trend over the last two decades

Source: Recof MARR Statistics. Green denotes In–In, Pink: In–Out, Blue: Out–In.

This change can be attributed to a number of factors, such as anti-trust deregulation in 1997, the introduction of share exchange system in 1999 and company separation system in 2000, and regulatory consolidated financial reporting that prompted many companies to review the portfolio of their businesses and subsidiaries. The post bubble period of choose and focus witnessed restructuring in many industries, as companies merged their subsidiaries, or regrouped them sometimes even with other companies in the same industry. Although it was then worried that M&A might destroy firm specific capabilities of the acquired firm, especially when the takeover is hostile, many companies found it favourable as it helped them increase market power, save tax, reduce redundancies and costs, form complementarities of assets and capabilities, and also access key competencies.

Studies showed that these M&A activities brought economic benefits. Okabe and Seki (2006), for example, using capital retention profitability, interest coverage and ROE as their measurement for the 157 M&As in 2001 that they analysed, showed that the M&As did have positive results, and thus could be considered as having contributed to Japan's economic restructure of that period. Miyajima (2006) too, upon inquiring the economic benefits of M&A, showed that it had positive effects on improving efficiency in organization and in resource allocation.

More recently, regardless of whether a subsidiary is acquired or newly established, a weak economy and a shrinking domestic market deemed it necessary for many firms to seek abroad for business growth prospects and markets. As shown in Figures 4 and 5 as well as in the Appendix, many companies are pursuing a group strategy and are using subsidiaries as their growth drivers. The management issue of controlling and coordinating with subsidiaries both domestic and foreign has become increasingly a vital issue to many large corporations in Japan.

Chapter 3

EVOLUTION OF THE JAPANESE CORPORATE SYSTEM

Before I begin my discussion on corporate groups in Japan, I find it appropriate, as a backdrop to the chapters that follow, to briefly describe the characteristics of the Japanese corporate system, and discuss how it has evolved or remain unchanged over what has been dubbed the "lost decades" since the economic bubble burst in 1991. I hope this will provide some context for understanding Japanese corporate groups.

In this chapter, I will romp through the changes in legal and institutional framework that have affected corporate groups in Japan. I will also describe how, during this period, we witnessed an increase in organizational diversity as firms strived to adapt to changes in different ways. And finally, I will discuss briefly whether the well-known community aspect of Japanese firms has withered in response to changes, and whether Japan's renowned skill regime still has a good fit with today's increasingly globalized, commoditized, and modularized business environment in many industries.

3.1 CHANGES IN LEGAL AND INSTITUTIONAL FRAMEWORK

Japan has changed dramatically over the past two decades, as firms strived to restructure themselves to be more competitive. Schaede (2008) wrote that 75% of 472 companies in the Nikkei 500 have engaged in at least one form of reorganization, namely, divestiture, consolidation or reorganization, and that 34% have adopted multiple measures. Schaede saw the period between 1998 and 2006 to be a "strategic inflection point" for Japanese businesses, a period when the competitive environment changed such that the balance of forces shifted away from previous ways of doing business to new ones. For example, from overemphasizing *shokunin* (ancient craftsmanship) and from being mass producers of high quality standardized products to being strategic providers of new product concepts with differentiated value proposition, and from making things to selling things. Many corporations urgently needed to reconfigure their capabilities and to evolve from being just producers to providers of full line services and solutions. As a senior manager at Hitachi, whom I have talked to, describes,

> "Many of our clients are governments, and being able to deliver top quality products is just not good enough when they are requiring full line services and solutions from product delivery to after maintenance and operations management, and when our major competitors are all proposing such total solutions."

Over the past few decades, there has been a series of related events that triggered what Schaede calls the inflection point. Liberalization of the financial market that began from 1980 enabled firms to raise capital from the market instead of relying on their main banks. Whittaker and Deakin (2009) described various pressures for change such as the weakening of bank-led monitoring, the decline of cross-shareholdings, the growth of foreign ownership and institutional shareholders, and the shrinking coverage of life time employment. There were many other changes too including accounting reforms as part of the financial Big Bang in 1996, the complete liberalization of corporate bond issuance in the same year, the introduction of share swap and transfer system in 1999 which triggered an unprecedented post war M&A and IPO boom, the relaxation of anti-trust law which enabled corporations to form pure holding companies, the revision of Company Law in 2002 which triggered corporate governance reforms, and the revision of Commercial Law in 2002, which made mandatory the disclosure of consolidated financial statement. Together, these changes in legal and institutional framework served as accelerator for changes in management style and organizational structure.

In considering the many institutional and organizational changes, one might speculate from a Varieties of Capitalism (VOC)[2] perspective that, facing pressures for change, Japan might move away from a coordinated market economy (CME) towards becoming a more liberal market economy (LME). Contrary to such expectations however, it appears that Japan has not quite converged towards LME. Vogel (2006), in his case study of eight Japanese firms, identified a distinctly Japanese approach towards corporate restructuring in which companies responded to cutting costs by exercising voice rather than exiting with long-term partners, including workers, banks, and suppliers. Japanese firms strived to adjust as much as possible without undermining cooperative relationships and to leverage these relationships to overcome their problems. Vogel saw Japan's transition as one that is different from both Japanese institutions of the past and U.S. institutions of the present, and that Japanese companies have re-evaluated their long-term relationships with worker, banks, and other firms, and

---

[2] Hall and Soskice categorized capitalist economies into two distinct types: liberal market economies (LME) and coordinated market economies (CME). In LMEs such as the US and the UK, firms coordinate their activities primarily via hierarchies, competitive market arrangements and formal contracting. In CMEs such as Germany and Japan, firms tend to depend more heavily on non-market relations, which entail more informal contracting and reliance on collaboration as opposed to competitive relationships. The VOC approach argues that the two types of economies have quite different capacities for innovation, with LMEs suitable for radical innovations whilst CMEs more suitable for incremental innovations. Variations can also be found within each type. For example northern European CMEs focus on industry-based coordination, whilst in Japan and South Korea group-based coordination is fostered.

that they have become more selective. But they have also become more differentiated and variable in their practices, and more open, as they have more foreign owners, managers, and business partners than ever before.

3.2 ADAPTIVE CHANGE AND ORGANIZATIONAL DIVERSITY

During this period of focus and change, firms adapted to changes in different ways and as a result we see an increase in diversity concerning organization types. From a corporate governance perspective, Jackson and Miyajima (2008) posited a typology of corporation types based on their analysis on survey data that were collected by the Policy Research Institute of the Ministry of Finance in 2003. This policy research itself too has indicated increasing diversity in the 1990s in organization structure, corporate governance and factors that fostered corporate group formation and expansion.

Their typology is based on cluster analysis which highlighted three common variables within the sampled firms. Namely, (a) market-oriented or relational finance and ownership, (b) outsider- or insider-oriented board and management, and (c) market-oriented or relational employment and incentive characteristics. Results suggest that Japanese firms fall into the following three broad groups.

- Traditional (J-type): Strong relational characteristics on all three dimensions. This type makes up 42% of the sample firms and 16% of employment.
- Hybrid model: Market finance but insider board and relational employment. (24% of sample firms and 67% of total employment)
- Intermediate: Relational finance or insider board, but with more market oriented employment. (34% of sample firms, 18% of employment)

It appears from the cluster analysis that the hybrid model, while being small in the number of firms, is becoming the predominant pattern amongst large Japanese firms. Miyajima (2011) noted, however, that this growth in diversity took place concurrently with a decline in the presence of Japan's leading companies within the global market. There were for example in 1995, 141 Japanese companies in the Fortune 500, making up 35.2% of the index's revenue share. The number of Japanese firms has since declined to 68 in 2008, and its revenue share fell to 11.2%. This decline in global presence and performance may have to do with the high costs that were incurred in the process of institutional transformation. Miyajima hypothesized that:

- The transition from an existing system to a new system (such as the hybrid type) may be hindered by organizational rigidity and lock-in, such that many firms find the process of restructuring and transformation to be slow.
- Change in organization architecture incurs coordination costs. For example, excessive power delegation may lead to control loss and wasteful redundancies in duplicated functions. The 2003 Policy Report by the Ministry of Finance also stated that the increase in corporate groups has led to significantly higher consolidated indirect costs, indicating duplication of corporate functions. On the other hand, insufficient power delegation also increases information processing costs. A lack of complementary institutions, such as effective monitoring to reduce agency costs, is also a factor that relates to poor performance.
- Hybrid arrangement incurs additional costs, such as the cost of selecting external board members, and the cost of giving up previous institutional complementarities. Dissolving cross-shareholdings would also dissolve risk sharing relationships.

Regarding how Japan has adapted to changes, although the organizational rigidity and isomorphism described above could be seen as what slows down change, it also reflects a quintessentially Japanese attitude towards western learning. Whittaker and Dean (2009) argued that a strong case can be made for the movement along the path in which executives seek to adapt producer capitalism to new circumstances. *Wakon Yosai* (harmonizing western brilliance with Japanese spirit) has historically been Japan's way towards adaptive change. They wrote that "Marketization, financialization, and global standards of accounting practices and corporate governance triggers change that is difficult to bring about endogenously for they are held in tension with existing norms and practices." Changes, therefore, have to be maintained with underlying continuity in the internal balances and implicit contracts of coordinated market capitalism.

Going back to the notion of Japan's non-convergence to LME, Aoki (2010), in addressing the issue of organizational rigidity from an inventive perspective, posed an interesting question that if there are differences in performance amongst different modes of organizational architecture, why then does a certain pattern of organizational architecture tend to appear as a national or regional convention even in markets for which it appears to be inappropriate? Aoki's work explained that different types of human cognitive assets of organizational relevance may co-evolve with corresponding organizational architectural modes. If a certain mode becomes the dominant mode of organizational architecture, the next generation of managers and workers tend to invest in the type of human assets that match that mode better, such that eventually that mode would become the established convention across all industries in that region even if it lacks comparative advantage. The next section looks at the resilience of a key characteristic of Japanese firms, namely community-ism.

3.3 RESILIENT COMMUNITY-ISM?

Community-ism, characterised by management and employees being important stakeholders of the firm, long-term or life-time employment, seniority-based wage system, and long-term development of firm-specific skills based on OJT, is a well-known aspect that can be recognized in many Japanese firms. Many literatures such as Dore (1973) have contrasted Japan's organization-oriented system, in which the firm belongs principally to the employees, who are its members, against the western market-oriented system in which shareholders, being owners, are principals, and managers are agents who contract at arm's length with employees who provide labour. In a typical Japanese community firm, the top management is not signifi-cantly constrained by either the board of directors, but is constrained, however, by its responsibilities as senior key members of the commu-nity. It is not surprising, therefore, that many adaptive changes came in the form of new Hybrid type firms, which use market finance, but yet continue to favour insider board and relational employment.

Given the many changes during this period, one might expect that the community characteristics of Japanese corporations would have changed too. Empirical research by Inagami and Whittaker (2005) over the period 1975–2000, showed, however, that there is little statistical evidence of the collapse of lifetime employment, and that the seniority-based pay, although weakened has not died. The principal means of developing skills is still through OJT. They, how-ever, hinted that this resilient Japanese model could be problematic if it fails to provide solutions for emerging issues, and warned that Japanese companies, being pushed relentlessly in the direction of high value added, knowledge-based, aesthetically creative products and services, need an employment system that can deliver these. In other words, there is a greater need in today's business environment for company professionals, who are expected to be not merely white col-lar support staff or supervisors to raise manufacturing efficiency, but to be sources and contributors of value added outputs.

Inagami and Whittaker also distinguished between creative workers and routine workers, and investigated whether the Japanese model of employment practices are compatible with the high expectations placed on employees. Interestingly, they found no fundamental con-tradiction between creative work and the classic Japanese model of employment practices. Contrary to popular view, Japanese creative workers do not change jobs frequently to seek more challenging work and higher wages. They have long-term employment orientations and a strong sense of affiliation with their company.

However, their survey did highlight some serious obstacles to working creatively, owing to poor work design and management, such as a lack of delegation of authority, frenetic work place, lack of support staff and long meetings. Managers who were asked the proportion of their employees who are engaged in creative work (defined as work that is not fixed and has a high discretionary content such that performance can vary greatly according to the individual and the output can have a major influence on the company), replied that the average is 32% in creative departments and 23% in routine departments. Employees themselves gave lower figures, 23% in creative departments and 20% in routine departments. In a community firm where reputation matters, and where the capability of taking on punishing amount of heavy work load gains recognition, departments are often chronically understaffed, such that workers have little time and energy left to invest in creative work.

From the empirical findings described above, one may conclude that the Japanese community firm model remains resilient as an established convention, and that it is compatible with creative work, but that work practices need to be changed to facilitate more creativity. Indeed in 2014, we witnessed some drastic changes in Japanese work practices amongst large Japanese corporate groups. The Nikkei newspaper[3] reported in July that for the first time in ten years Sony has revised its HR and wage policies in 2014. A job grade system is to be introduced in 2015 that would link pay to the importance and contribution of defined job grades, thus promoting motivation whilst lowering total wage costs. The traditional *nenko* system (wage rise based on seniority) will be abolished. Panasonic too announced that from October onwards, it will abolish its *nenko* system and further enhance its performance related pay. Like Sony, wage will depend on the importance of the job position's role. Likewise, Hitachi also announced similar measures in September. These measures address a wage distortion problem that many Japanese manufacturers face, where unlike factory workers whose skills and craftsmanship develop with their years of experience, under the *nenko* system, the value added that is created by the white collar employees is often below the wage level.

---

[3] The Nijon Keizai Shinbun on-line version: 25th July Sony revises HR and wage for the first time in ten years to rectify high costs; 30th July Panasonic abolishes *nenko* system and revises wage structure for the first time in ten years; 26th September Hitachi abolishes *nenko* system and creates a global standard wage system; 27th September Hitachi, Fujitsu and others to introduce common global HR evaluation system, with the aim of acquiring global talent.

The need for a wide pool of talent with new ideas and cultural intelligence also means that many Japanese firms are looking into sourcing global talent. If the performance of creative value added work depends more on individual capability, then firms will need to be able to negotiate wages individually. But under the *nenko* system where employees are compensated at a later phase of their career, it is hard for firms to hire talented young staffs because of the relatively low and uncompetitive wage levels. The abolishment of the *nenko* system would, therefore, give Japanese firms more room to source talent globally. However, it should also be noted that such labour mobility and the creation of positional good (as there are only limited positions in a company that could now guarantee a pay rise) could potentially disrupt communityism if employees see the change as a breach of psychological contract, or if they feel that the distribution process of such positional goods is not done fairly. Such negative perception could dampen employee motivation and increase internal transaction costs of the company.

3.4 SHIFT IN COMPARATIVE ADVANTAGE

Another aspect of many Japanese firms is their emphasis on "*suria-wase*" or working through coordination. This may be coordination with suppliers, sub-contractors, subsidiaries or other entities within the firm's value production network. However, it has been noted that this systems, which has hitherto worked well, is no longer effective in some industries. Motohashi (2003) wrote that the Japanese relational model, which tend to stress information sharing, is effective in sectors, such as automobile, where different divisions are highly complementary in the decision making process and hence *suriawase* (coordination) is required. But in sectors such as electronics where the degree of modularity increases and speedy innovation is required, coordination in this relational model often becomes an obstacle and does not work well. Referring to Nonaka and Takeuchi's SECI model, which describes a spiral of knowledge creation from tacit to tacit, tacit to explicit, explicit to explicit, explicit to tacit, Motohashi noted that Japanese firms are relatively good at externalizing (creation of formal knowledge from tacit knowledge) and using tacit knowledge, but they do not make effective use of formal knowledge outside the company, and are thus especially weak in the area of combination, such as productive development in cooperation with outside organizations.

A shift to a more modularized industrial world would mean that there are now sectors of the economy where the Japanese model still continues to offer comparative advantage, and sectors where it does not. To be able to compete successfully, it is important that Japanese corporations formulate strategies that embrace more speed and collaboration.

3.5 SHIFT IN REQUIRED SKILLS AND SKILL FORMATION

Shifts in comparative advantage also imply a shift in required skills, while skill formation depends on the skill regime of the country. Coordinated market economies (CME) such as Japan tend to have highly skilled employees with task-specific or industry-specific skills working with low-risk institutional employment protection such as life-time employment. They are, therefore, more likely to be able to support organizational strategies requiring incremental improvements to product lines provided by contributions from employees throughout the organizational hierarchy. On the other hand, in liberal market economies (LME) where radical innovations are critical, competition is often cost based, and first mover advantage plays an important part in firm success. Employment security and protection tend to be much weaker in LMEs, but, in turn, institutional structures support the development of portable and generic skills.

In many industries where radical innovation is a required key competence, having a CME skill regime may be a handicap because innovation is often incremental. Hall and Soskice (2001) argued that national institutional environments differ in their capability to meet organizational demands for radical or incremental innovations. Regarding CMEs, Whitley *et al.* (2003) wrote that:

> Firms that encourage key staff to develop organization-specific, generalist, skills and knowledge through long term careers, as in Japan, find

it difficult to attract and retain highly skilled specialists who seek to enhance their generic competences on external labour markets.... Developing new organization-wide capabilities through incorporating the knowledge and skills of overseas subsidiaries into novel managerial routines is more problematic. ... This also suggests that companies with generalist career structures may be at some disadvantage in industries primarily organized around project teams composed of specialized experts in highly fluid labour markets.

So to what extent are these claims true? And if true, are firms aware of such shifts in comparative advantage and required skills? The 16th Corporate White Paper (2009) of the *Keizai Doyukai* still states a strong bottom-up frontline-ism based on long-term employment and relational trust to be their major core competence. But many firms and institutions including the METI are acutely aware of areas where the Japanese model no longer works well, especially areas that have ceded substantial global share in recent years.

Yanagawa *et al.* (2009) attributed the limitations of the Japanese model to an over reliance on firm specific skills. They argued that having exceptional proprietary skills is insufficient if the firm is slow in bringing the product to market, and if prices are not competitive. Although many Japanese firms claim to have strong firm specific skills, which in themselves are not always related to productivity, they often lack professional or industry skills that are required to complement firm specific skills. This is worrisome, especially in light of Japan's ageing population, more innovation and value-added activities are needed to raise Japan's TFP.

What exactly are Japanese firm specific skills? And how do Japanese companies perceive capabilities and competencies? Except for manufacturing technicians, most managerial white collars' skills are quite general and broad in nature, even though they are often labelled as firm specific. Busemeyer (2009) wrote that in the case of Japan, firms engage in the formation of broad occupational skills and try to reduce labour mobility at the same time. Japan's firm-based skill regime is Williamsonian rather than Beckerian in that it is firm-specific in the sense of more bilateral dependency rather than narrower and fewer skills. Bilateral dependency arises for the firm because the worker could leave and try to sell his or her skills to another employer. The worker on the other hand, depends on the firm's willingness to value his or her investments in specific skills by paying higher wages.

This bilateral dependency is sustained also because of adverse selection. Asao (2004) posited that because of information asymmetries, the market wage is often the weighted average of talented skilled workers and poorly skilled workers, such that the former would prefer to remain in the company rather than accepting the average market wage, and thus leaving the market with workers of poorer quality. Because the company is able to benefit from this surplus as long as wage is below marginal productivity, the company will have the incentive to invest in both firm-specific as well as general skills. Two equilibria emerge as outcomes of such information asymmetries concerning the quality of workers. One in which there is high labour mobility and under-investment in skills because when mobility is high, the risk of workers leaving with skills invested by the firm will also be high, and another in which there is low labour mobility and a high level of investment in skills.

One might assume that in a generous welfare state like Japan, workers will be more willing to invest in more firm specific skills, because social security mitigates the labour market risks associated with investments in firm specific skills that has little market value. But with such reduced risks, it would also then be easier for workers to change jobs, such that higher levels of labour mobility lower firms' willingness to invest in training. But in Japan, as pointed out by Miwa (2006) and Yanagawa (2009), the life-time employment provided by firms, acts as providers of social security, and such predominance of company-based welfare policies has prevented the emergence of a generous welfare state. This may explain why Japan's firm-based skill regime is Williamsonian, in other words bilaterally dependant.

With the two equilibria that can be expected from the bilateral dependency of Japan's firm specificity, it appears that equilibrium has in recent years tilted more towards higher labour mobility and under-investment by firms in general skills. Under-investment by workers in general skills also causes firms too to reduce investment in firm-specific skills because of the complementarity nature of both skills.

1 billion yen

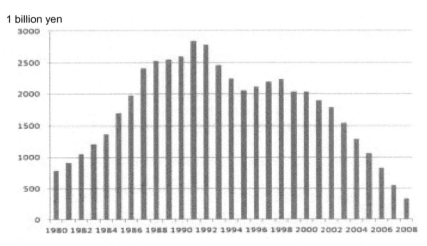

Figure 7: Investment in OFF-JT by firms (manufacturing and non-manufacturing combined)

Source: Cabinet office statistics report 2012.

According to statistics from the Cabinet's Office,[4] firms appear to have reduced investments in OFF-JTs as shown in Figure 7.

It is not just mobility that has caused firms to cut back on OFF-JT investments. Many firm's HR practices have changed too in times when training budgets are tight, and where long-term employment was being criticized. Heavy emphasis was placed in the 90s on employees being responsible for their own skill development. It was considered ideal that employees should invest in portable skills that they could use when they consider changing jobs. Some firms, as shown in the Ministry of Health, Labour and Welfare's 2012 annual skill development survey, did, however, urge their employees to develop skills based on job skill requirement that is consistent with the firm's strategy. This trend hopefully would lead to the development of firm specific skills that are less generic and more focused on skills that would enable the firm to compete effectively. Although some firms appear to be progressing well, many

---

[4]Working Group Report on the State of the Japanese Economy and Policies, Document 2-2, p. 5.

firms are still struggling to re-adjust their HR policies. A recent report by the Ministry of Health, Labour and Welfare revealed that 68% of companies have problems with human resource and skill development, and that these problems lie in both training and in evaluating skills. Whether companies can indeed succeed in training their employees and equipping them with required skills will be extremely crucial not just to the companies concerned but to Japan's economy as a whole.

Chapter 4

WHY DO CORPORATE GROUPS EXIST?

In trying to understand the phenomena of Japanese companies' increasing use of subsidiaries, and the economic rationale for doing so, this chapter looks at several theories such as the transaction cost theory, the property rights approach, the resource-based view, and the contingency theory-based view, as well as empirical research on Japanese corporate groups.

4.1 THE COASIAN QUESTION REVISITED — TRANSACTION COST AND BOUNDARY OF THE FIRM

Traditional firm theory posits that firms exist because it is costly to use the pricing system to coordinate economic activity. Ronald Coase (1960) and Oliver Williamson (1985) highlighted costs, such as cost of finding transaction partners, cost of negotiation and renegotiation (because most contracts are by nature incomplete), and cost of writing and enforcing contracts that are involved in using the pricing system, as well as the role organizations play in reducing such transaction costs. Coase's model shows that when the external transaction costs are higher than the internal transaction costs, the company will grow. This can be seen as a market failure situation where market governance is replaced by hierarchical governance. If however, the external transaction costs are lower than the internal transaction costs the company will downsize by outsourcing. By doing so, the company can reduce the cost of coordinating among divisions.

For Williamson, the existence of firms derives from asset specificity in production. Firm specific assets cause problems if the assets are owned by different firms because both agents are likely to be locked into a position where they are no longer competing with a number of agents in the market, such that ex-post opportunistic behaviour may arise. Transaction costs may further increase if the transaction concerned is complex and bears uncertainties, such that re-negotiation may be necessary. Where transaction costs are deemed to be high, firms will have the incentive to save transaction costs by having full ownership over those firm specific assets through vertical integration.

The fundamental choice among governance mechanism is whether to externally organise transactions outside the boundary of the firm in the market, or whether to internally organise transactions within the firm's boundaries. In transaction cost economics, the mode of governance therefore reflects the type of transaction. For transactions that are of high frequency and long periods, that are complex and have high uncertainty, that are hard to evaluate and measure, that are related to other assets and production such that changes require difficult coordination beyond firm boundary, relational contract or in-house transaction is often the preferred mode of governance. This relationship between the modes of governance and the types of transactions is shown in Figure 8.

In real life situations however, firm boundary is often less straight forward. An empirical research by Shinya (2008) on car manufacturers in Japan showed, for example, that correlation between complexity and vertical integration can be both positive and negative depending on the issue at stake. Increased complexity in car manufacturing and assembly increased coordination costs with suppliers of auto parts and this caused car manufacturers to further integrate, thus conforming to the Coasian expectation. However, increased complexity also caused some manufacturers to reduce integration and rely more on specialized suppliers. Some manufacturers

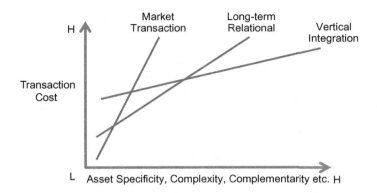

Figure 8:   Asset specificity, transaction cost and mode of transaction

respond to increased complexity by switching from specialized parts to standardized and modularized parts that can easily be specified and evaluated, thus reducing transaction costs.

Firm boundary may also be grey when we consider a corporate group in which the parent–subsidiary relationship can be quasi-market like, yet maintains formal or informal ties to the corporate hierarchy. A subsidiary can behave like a virtual internal department taking orders from the corporate group headquarters, or it can be involved in a long-term relational contracts, or it can be treated by the corporate headquarters as merely one of many suppliers in the market. Or a subsidiary can be an intermediate hybrid organization where both features of hierarchical control and market transaction co-exist.

It is perhaps this intermediate nature of subsidiaries that could possible explain the rationale for using them. K. Ito (1995) posited that this form of governance balances two transaction costs simultaneously. The argument is that if a parent company has complete control over its subsidiary, its excessive interference may restrict productivity and hinder growth of the subsidiary. On the other hand, if the parent chooses market transaction, costs may become prohibitively high. Having quasi-market transactions with subsidiaries, therefore, balance the costs associated with external market transaction and costs associated with internal transaction. Figure 9 illustrates the potential cost balance advantage of using subsidiaries.

Parent Company	Subsidiary Company	Market Transaction
Choose in-house when external TC (transaction cost) is high. But then excessive control by management may also reduce productivity and increase costs. Cost of integration may outweigh TC.	Choose subsidiary when it is better to balance internal and external transaction costs, as well as to balance control rights.	Choose market when transaction costs are lower, and when there is little risk of *ex-post* opportunistic behaviour or uncertainties. In many cases, the cost of using the market can be prohibitively high.

Figure 9:   Choice between in-house, subsidiary, and market

But does this rationale hold for all types of subsidiaries? I argue that this would depend on the type of subsidiary. For example, if a subsidiary is a manufacturing unit that supplies machine parts solely to its parent company, such that the relationship requires more control than an individual business spinoff subsidiary, then balancing control may be less an issue, while balancing the cost of transferring tacit knowledge, which may be cheaper inside the firm, and labour costs, which may be cheaper outside the firm, could be a more plausible rationale. We will examine this issue later in this book when we look at different balances in different types of subsidiaries.

4.2 PROPERTY RIGHTS APPROACH

Another rationale as to why firms form corporate groups and have ownership over subsidiary companies can be understood from property rights approach (Grossman and Hart, 1986, and Hart and Moore, 1990). When it is too costly for one firm to specify in a contract a long list of specific rights it desires over another firm's assets, it may be efficient *ex ante* to purchase all the rights except for those specifically mentioned in the contract. Ownership is essentially the purchase of these residual rights.

According to their theory, ownership matters when the relationship specific investment is important, and when there exist different opportunities in utilizing firm assets and relation specific assets. If the parent company of a 100% owned subsidiary has claims to its residual returns, the parent will have the incentive to invest in and provide training to the subsidiary. If it is not a subsidiary, such investments in training would be economically inefficient as it would only increase the seller's quasi-rent. Also when there are high uncertainties or when the contract is incomplete (as most contracts are), resource allocation can be more efficient by having residual control rights over various asset utilization options.

It follows that if returns on relation specific human assets are high, the parent company will choose to own and use its subsidiary. If on the other hand, returns are lower than returns from general human assets, the firm will outsource instead. It is important to note here that relation specific human assets such as management and employee skills create value only when they are used in conjunction with related assets. Whether or not to own such related assets depends on whether the assets are independent or strictly complementary. When the related assets such as retail stores and delivery systems are independent, it is desirable for each firm to own their specific assets (e.g. marketing and product development capability). This is because if one party takes over ownership of all assets, the merged party, seeing any further investment as action that would increase the other party's quasi rent at its own expense, may cease to invest in relation specific assets. In other words, it could distort incentives and create efficiency losses sufficiently to make common ownership harmful. On the other hand, when it is desirable for one firm to own both sets of assets as in the case of a merger, the assets likely to be complementary and not independent, and hence owning the assets will increase the value of the firm's relation specific investments. Assets are said to be strictly complementary when, without employing both assets, relation specific assets do not create value.

Remember in the previous section, we touched on K. Ito's (1996) posited rationale of using subsidiaries to balance internal and external transaction costs. Following that rationale, ownership is good only when the parent company's control increases the productivity of management more than the decrease in the subsidiary's productivity resulting from the subsidiary's loss of control. Or when the quasi-market, which balances ownership, effectively lowers the otherwise potentially high costs allocating control rights exclusively to one party would incur. However, when situations occur that makes such a balance impractical, such as when a conflict of interests between shareholders slows down the parent company's strategy execution, a sell off or a 100 percent ownership may be preferable.

Although it would appear that ownership provides residual rights of control, and, therefore, enlarges the range of actions open to the owner company, it should be noted also that the owner cannot commit himself to intervene only selectively in its subsidiary's operations. This is because by their very definition, residual rights refer to powers that cannot be specified *ex ante*. Integration can, therefore, impose costs as well as benefits.

4.3 RESOURCE-BASED VIEW

Some academics argue that the incentive-based transaction cost theory, as described in the previous sections, has been made to carry too much weight in explaining the theory of organizations. For example, Langlois and Foss (1997) pointed out that this tends to "reduce virtually all problems of economic organization to problems of misaligned incentives attendant on imperfect information." In what they called generically the "capabilities view", they added two more theoretical avenues to the incentive alignment approach. One is the possibility that knowledge about how to produce is imperfect, and the second is the possibility that knowledge about how to link together productive knowledge with that of another is also imperfect. They proposed that the fundamental role of an organization is to help cooperating parties to align not just their incentives, but also their knowledge. Foss (1996) added, however, that there is complementarity between the incentive theory and the capabilities view in that the full realization of the rent-yielding potential of capabilities requires incentives that harmonize the actions of resource owners and provide stimuli to invest in the accumulation of human capital.

Some of the main arguments under the resource based view are that productive activity requires the cooperation and coordination of teams of resources, where routines are to the organization what skills are to the individual. Organizational routines involve a large component of tacit knowledge (Grant, 1991). Organizational routines are firm specific assets assembled in integrated clusters spanning individuals or groups so that they enable distinctive activities to be carried out. Dynamic capabilities refer to the firm's ability to integrate, build and reconfigure internal and external competencies to address rapidly changing environments (Teece, 1997). Managers, when building core competencies, decide whether to make or buy needed inputs (Prahalad and Hamel, 1990). Competencies should be durable and inimitable; in other words they should not be transparent, transferable and replicable (Grant, 1991).

Individuals and organizations are limited in what they know how to do well, and in a world of tacit knowledge, having the same blueprints as one's competitors is unlikely to translate into having the same costs of production. In addition, capabilities are not bound to individual input-owners but are tied to clusters of interacting input-owners. Knowledge is also not universal because of social embeddedness. Tacit knowledge therefore makes trading of capabilities difficult. A key implication here is that capabilities may be a crucial factor that determines what will be done in the organization and what by the market. In other words, capabilities may determine the boundaries of firm.

Because of cognitive constraints, all organizations need to specialize, and the costs of integrating across diverse capabilities may become so high that they may outweigh external transaction costs. The organizational question is whether new capabilities are best acquired through the market, through internal learning, or through some hybrid organizational form such as subsidiaries. It is however not easy to discern the extent to which firms consciously draw their boundaries based on capabilities.

The statistics below on Japanese firms show a rather mixed picture of make or buy. The METI 2007 White Paper, which collected data from a sample of 140,000 firms in the manufacturing industry, shows that there are multiple layers of transactions. 773 firms listed in the first section of the Tokyo Exchange have transactions directly or indirectly with around 80,000 firms (directly with 40,880 first tier firms, directly or indirectly with 29,305 second tier firms, and 12,032 with third to sixth tier firms). Depending on the manufacturing sector, the internal transaction rate within this vertically integrated chain ranges from 33% to a high 86%, with an average of 57%. The data, however, does not show the number of subsidiary companies within the tiers, though it is reasonable to assume that they include both subsidiaries and non-subsidiaries.

Looking also again at the annual Basic Survey of Corporate Activities (*Kigyou Katsudo Kihon Chousa*) conducted by METI as of 31st March 2012, in which data were collected from 29,570 firms, 45.1% of the surveyed firms reported outsourcing for manufacturing, and 43.7% for purposes other than manufacturing, while 33.6% replied that they do not outsource. Areas of non-manufacturing outsourcing are shown in Table 5.

Of the total amount paid for manufacturing outsourcing, 39.9% of total payments were paid to affiliated companies. For non-manufacturing outsourcing, 35.5% of total payments were paid to affiliated companies. There is, therefore, a mixed usage of both outsourcing and affiliated companies. Whether this combination of usage reflects Japanese companies' conscious decision on balancing costs of integrating capabilities and transaction costs is not known, and this may, therefore, be a subject for further investigation. But should it be the case that Japan, which is renowned for its cooperative capitalism, and Japanese companies for their strength in *suriawase* or co-production through

Table 5: Percentage of firms that outsourcing for various activities

Logistics	46.7%
Environment and security	44.3%
Specialized areas such as accounting and tax	35.6%
Information systems related	35.1%
Routine general office work	24.9%
Employee training	18.8%
Employee welfare and fringe benefit related	12.8%
Survey and marketing	11.8%
Design and product development	11.1%
R&D related	10.8%
Public relations	4.9%
Others	24.0%

the sharing of tacit-knowledge, are allowing their costs of knowledge integration go unchecked, this could then be a worrisome situation.

4.4 ORGANIZATIONAL DESIGN PERSPECTIVE — CONTINGENCY THEORY-BASED VIEW

Contingency theory posits that there is no best way to organize a corporation, and that the optimal course of action is contingent upon the company's internal and external environment. The organization of production activities into a corporate group system consisting of a parent company and its subsidiaries can be understood as a matter of organizational design in response to existing environments. Kali (2002), for example, posited that activities are more costly to measure subjectively the further they are located from the core firm, and that organizational design is often tailored in response to the best relational contract. Enright and Subramanian (2012) wrote that the types of subsidiaries and their roles within a corporate group have often been regarded by researchers as second-order effects deriving primarily from an overall strategy choice.

Another organizational structure approach can be seen in the analytical framework of Aoki and Okuno (1996). According to their model, in situations where different operational divisions are highly complementary, the most advantageous institution is one in which the different divisions engage extensively in information sharing, while devolving decision making power to the level of shop floor. On the other hand, in situations where different operational divisions are not highly complementary, and where it is not necessary to invest in coordination, the most advantageous institution features centralised top–down decision making.

4.4.1 Subsidiary as a Means to Solve Incentive and Commitment Problems

In response to a need to motivate business units to invest in their specialized areas of business, hiving-off business units into subsidiary companies is a strategy that can be used to solve incentive problems that often accompany decentralization. A CEO, in his or her desire to induce employees to make firm specific investments, may delegate power to employees, but then the CEO may also renege on his or her promise, and interfere *ex-post* with the decisions made by the employees. The employees, foreseeing this *ex-ante*, will lose incentive to make firm specific investments. Ito, Kikutani and Hayashida (1997), posited that one way to resolve this type of incentive problem is to reinforce commitment by hiving off departments or business units into separate legal entities in the form of subsidiaries. Hiving off increases independent-ness and accountability of the subsidiary, turned, business units, and also speeds up decision making, which is often required in fast changing business environments.

In their empirical study, a field research was done on six large corporate groups, and a survey on 849 manufacturing firms. From the survey results, as shown in Table 6, we can see the reasons corporate groups give for hiving out. It can be observed that many firms actively use hiving off strategies to enhance incentives.

Table 6:   Reasons for hiving-off

1. To specialize and allocate resource to on business with growth potential	51%
2. To strengthen management of the corporate group	41%
3. To separate businesses and transactions of different nature	21%
4. To be clear about responsibility and accountability	20%
5. To slim down parent company as part of restructuring effort	19%
6. To expand manufacturing and sales to other regions	18%
7. To facilitate business with firms outside the corporate group	18%
8. To enhance power delegation	13%
9. To secure employment	12%
10. To reduce labour costs	11%
11. To confine risks in new business venture to the subsidiary	10%
12. To implement labour practices that are different from that of the parent company	10%
13. To separate unprofitable businesses	3%
14. To benefit from tax and finance	2%
15. Other reasons	11%

Source: Ito, Hayashida, Kikutani (1997).

The idea that excessive control creates incentive problems that reduces productivity and hence incur high internal transaction costs, is essentially why control needs to be balanced by using the quasi-market transaction in the form of subsidiaries .

4.4.2 Other Empirical Evidence on Company Preferences

Based on another survey which was conducted in 2007, Aoki and Miyajima (2011) showed the preferences companies have towards internal organization versus completely owned subsidiary. The results are summarised in Table 7. Companies appear to recognize the merits of using subsidiaries for being able to make possible the usage of multiple and hence flexible wage patterns, enhance responsibility and accountability, speed up decision making thus making it possible to respond more quickly to customer demand and market conditions. On the other hand however, companies appear to favour internal organizations because coordination of activities across departments is easier than coordinating with subsidiary companies. The results show that there is a trade-off between the benefits of decentralization and control losses in the choice of organizational architecture.

Table 7: Merits of using internal organization versus completely owned subsidiary

	n	Internal (%)	Subsidiary (%)
Merits of using subsidiaries			
Flexible usage of labour cost structure	167	7.2	64.1
Clear accountability, monitoring costs	169	13.6	42.0
Speed in decision making	169	21.3	42.0
Quick response to customer market demand	169	12.4	41.4
Merits of using internal organization			
Consolidated basic strategy	169	53.3	8.3
Coordination between organizations	168	48.8	14.9
Ease of HR transfers within organization	169	47.3	17.2
Synergies between business units	169	33.1	7.1
Ease of business restructuring	169	32.5	27.8
Utilization of production facilities	166	25.9	12.7
Efficient allocation of finances	169	25.4	10.7

Adapted from Aoki and Miyajima (2011).

In a more recent survey on 3,444 companies, Morikawa (2012) described that 60.8% of the companies that have used hiving off strategies gave clear accountability and responsibility as their reason: 27.3% gave quicker decision making, 21% gave cost reduction, and 19% gave sales expansion as their reasons. When asked whether performance has improved after hiving-off business units into subsidiaries, 2/3 of the companies replied that "performance has improved" or "performance has generally improved".

4.4.3 Subsidiary as a Response to Diversification

From their survey data, Aoki and Miyajima also investigated the drivers of decentralization. Using the level of decentralization as the dependent variable, and diversification, globalization, organization structure as independent variables, controlled for company size and industry sector, they conducted an OLS regression. The model showed that of the independent variables, diversification (entropy index) best explains (at 1% significant level) what drives companies to delegate power to business units. A similar model was established to test power delegation to subsidiary companies. Again, decentralization is used as the dependent variable, whilst globalization, group formation and organization structure were used as independent variables, controlled for company size and industry sector. Here too, results show that diversification explains (at 5% significant level) power delegation to subsidiary companies.

However, rather contrary to expectations, the relationship between the level of group formation and power delegation was not identified. This may be due to the *rentan* ratio (consolidated revenue divided by non-consolidated revenue of the parent company) that was used to operationalize the measurement of group formation. The use of *rentan* ratio as a measurement of group formation is appropriate only when most of the subsidiaries are individual revenue generating businesses different from the parent's core business, such that more subsidiaries would lead to a higher *rentan* ratio. But if subsidiaries are mainly functional ones in the sense they are suppliers within the value chain of the parent's core business, their trading revenue within the group are netted and will not therefore affect the *rentan* ratio. It is possible that a large corporate group may have expanded to have hundreds of functional subsidiaries, but yet have a low *rentan* ratio.

4.4.4 Subsidiary as a Means of Fulfilling the Community Firm's Commitments

In Chapter 3, we saw that the community aspect of Japanese firms has remained relatively resilient despite adaptive response to changes in business and institutional environment. In a community firm, its internal labour market is not necessarily a market where information is complete and where staff talent and staff needs are matched efficiently. As Dore (2000) described, "the so called internal labour market is internal but not market as people are posted by HR rather than through competition for vacancies." Subsidiaries are often used as a means to absorb the parent's labour. This is not necessarily because labour is redundant, but because within the community firm, it is necessary to find positions for competent employees when positions available are limited in the parent company. And as K. Ito (1996) described, many subsidiaries are created as "places to reallocate some employees from the parent firm. This occurs because there are only a limited number of available positions at upper management levels in any organization."

This practice of reallocation may be based on the embedded presumption that these elite and experienced generalists are indeed competent employees. But as firms diversify to unrelated businesses in which these firm specific generalists have little knowledge of, especially as these generalists are often former division managers who would have imbibed parent company's work culture rather than corporate officers equipped with management experience and competence required for the business. This community-purposed reallocation may cause serious problems to the subsidiaries concerned.

In this chapter, I have shown some of the major theories and empirical research from existing literatures that can be applied to explain why subsidiaries exist and why they are preferred to market transactions as well as to internal business divisions. We looked at how a subsidiary's quasi-market transaction can be used to balance high transactions costs in using the market and high internal costs that hierarchical transaction incurs. We looked at the importance of owning subsidiaries and hence residual rights when there are multiple opportunities in using the assets and when there is uncertainty and incomplete contracts, and also when residual returns on relation specific human assets are high, which then motivates the parent to invest in such assets. Returns however depend on whether the related assets are independent or complementary. Here again, a quasi-market is effective if there are high costs involved in allocating control rights solely to one party. We looked also at how tacit knowledge which is costly to transfer, and which may outweigh transaction costs, can determine whether activities should be performed within the corporate group or outsourced. And finally, we looked at how the design and choice of organization are contingent upon internal and external environments.

Although the theories and empirical literatures that I have referred to in this chapter are not exhaustive, I believe they are sufficient at least in highlighting from an economic rationale point of view, the intermediary characteristic of subsidiaries that lie between market and in-house transaction, and ways in which firms could take advantage of this characteristic to optimize their organization contingent upon existing internal and external environment.

Chapter 5

HOW ARE SUBSIDIARY COMPANIES MANAGED?

In this chapter, we will be looking at various aspects of subsidiary management. One may perhaps imagine that in a large and diversified corporate group, certain amount of decision rights need to be delegated to its subsidiaries, otherwise it would be undesirably slow and prohibitively costly to make all decisions centrally. Delegation however incurs control loss, and the parent company, therefore, has to decide on a workable level of delegation that is optimal. Another management issue would be the coordination of activities across the corporate group. If what the subsidiary performs is highly integrated into the production value chain of the parent company, delegation may have to be balanced with appropriate control to ensure that targets of the group as a whole are met. Monitoring of performance may vary in frequency and detail, and evaluation criteria may be financial or non-financial. Conflict management may also be an issue, such as when the parent and subsidiary face different pressures and have conflicting interests. There also needs to be some form of self-enforcement to allow members within the corporate group to act coherently. In the subsequent sections, I will look at each of these management issues and see how academic literatures address them.

5.1 DELEGATION OF POWER

With increasing globalization, diversification, complexity of business activities, and a need for greater accountability, as well as a need to develop core competencies that fuel growth in new businesses, many Japanese firms have choosen to decentralize decision making by delegating power to subsidiary companies. However, there are costs and benefits related to decentralization. Mookherjee (2005) wrote that costs of communication and information can indeed be lowered through decentralization, but this may lead to power abuse and loss of control. With some departures from the revelation principle, Mookherjee showed that incentive problems can be overcome by judicious design of a delegation arrangement. According to him, conditions for delegation to be optimal are (a) Observability of sub-contract costs or allocation, (b) Top–down contracting, and (c) Risk neutrality and absence of limited liability constraints. In the absence of these incentive problems, coordination across different units can be achieved by a hierarchical communication system that resembles a management accounting system. A parent company can, for example, contract with Subsidiary X to select profit targets. Subsidiary X report costs or bid on projects to its parent company after receiving cost reports from its subordinate Subsidiary Y. The parent company then could aggregate all information and make an output decision that would again flow down the hierarchy to its subsidiaries. Mookherjee posited that any hierarchy that is consistent with the above conditions can achieve the same expected results as the optimal centralized outcomes. Although the conditions that are described for achieving optimality of delegation are very restrictive, it is nonetheless interesting to note that this technology described by Mookherjee resembles very much the kind of bottom-up planning known as "*tsumiage*" used in many Japanese companies, where lower layers of the hierarchy report budget plans, which would be used by the subsequent layer to report to its next higher layer, whilst all the budget targets are based on instruction given by top management. If we do not have the technology described by Mookherjee, then it is necessary to assume that delegation involves incentive costs. And if such costs are substantial, the choice between centralization and decentralization will involve trade-offs between high incentive costs of delegation (or loss of control if incentives fail) and benefits of delegation such as communication, information processing and flexibility of production decision.

Another insight from Mookherjee is the superiority of decentralization in obtaining local information which cannot be accessed by a central mechanism. This is because of information restrictions. Mookherjee reasoned that if upper bound on the size of message space is not large enough to permit agents to communicate everything they know, centralized decision making cannot access all the information that delegation mechanism utilizes. If decentralization is indeed superior, then this poses a problem to group management practices in Japan where delegation of decision rights to subsidiaries are often limited, and important decisions are made by the parent company.

Although subsidiaries have access to valuable local information, as the information moves up the hierarchy to the parent company, they become more selective because of size restriction, such that the top layer could only have access to a very abridged version of all information. In the course of selection, it is also possible that selection error will occur such that important information fails to be transmitted. Knowing what information to select and process is, therefore, a very important coordination issue. Hence it is important, firstly, to delegate decision rights to an appropriate level in the organization which has the capability to act according to the management's intention whilst making use of local information to improve decision making. A senior manager seconded or transferred from the parent company to the subsidiary may effectively fulfil this role, and this practice is actually widely used in Japanese corporate groups. Secondly, it is also important to maintain a system that ensures the quality of information that flows up the hierarchy to the management. For example, a company that I have talked to said they mandate the inclusion of risk information when transmitting information up the hierarchy.

Because the optimal location of decision rights involves a trade-off between agency costs and knowledge transfer costs, including delays, such as in moving information to the individual who possesses the decision rights, firm exhibit preferences on the extent and the kind of decision rights that should be delegated. In their empirical research, Zoghi and Mohr (2007) identified that company size is strongly related to decision rights. In larger establishments where information transmission can be much slower, decisions are more likely to be delegated. There is, however, difference in types of decisions that are particularly likely to be decentralized. There are firm characteristics such as firm size and complexity of required knowledge that increase how long it may take to make decisions, and firm characteristics such as inability to monitor workers that increase agency costs. There are also characteristics such as strong unions and use of information technologies that affect both time taken in decision making and agency costs. These characteristics affect the choice of distribution of decision rights.

Regarding the extent of power delegation, Ito, Kikutani, and Hayashida (1997) showed in their empirical research that on average the extent (measured by survey data on whether the parent company or subsidiary gets to make decisions) is greater in a parent–subsidiary setting than in a head-office-business division setting. Power delegation is also greater in cases where personnel connections are relatively weak (measured by percentage of board member and employee secondments and transfers from the parent company), where ownership by parent company is less than 50%, where subsidiaries use external finance, and for strategic decisions, where subsidiaries are horizontally integrated instead of being vertically integrated. The study also showed varying degrees of delegation depending on the activity concerned. For example, power delegation shows to be higher in operational decisions than in strategic decisions.

A more recent empirical research was conducted by Miyajima in conjunction with the Research Institute of Economy Trade and Industry (RIETI) and the Ministry of Economy Trade and Industry (METI), in which 251 companies were surveyed. Consistent with Ito *et al.*'s findings, Miyajima also identified varying degrees of power delegation dependent on the activity concerned. As shown in Figure 10, subsidiaries appear to have more autonomy than business units, and that although subsidiaries have decision rights over HR (except for

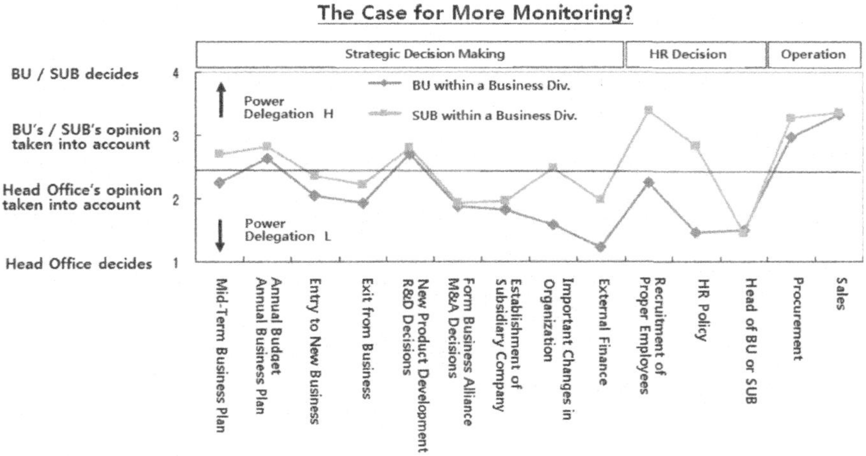

The Case for More Monitoring?

Figure 10: Comparison of power delegation to business divisions and subsidiaries
Source: RIETI Miyajima (2007).

top personnel) and operational decisions, many strategic decision-making still remain in the hands of the corporate head-office.

5.2 COMPLETE OWNERSHIP

In Chapter 4, we discussed from a property right's approach that ownership of assets that are used in conjunction with relation specific human assets creates value when the assets complement each other, and that when there are high costs to allocating control rights exclusively to the parent company, using a quasi-market in the form of subsidiaries is effective. Given that subsidiaries can be used to balance control, it is interesting to observe a contrary trend where many parent companies are increasing control over their subsidiaries by having 100% ownership as shown in Figure 10. According to a survey conducted by Teikoku Databank, a company that specializes in collecting and analysing corporate data, of the 649 companies that were delisted from the stock exchange market in Japan for the period commencing from 2005 to July 2009, 341 (53%) was a result of parent companies acquiring full ownership of their subsidiaries.

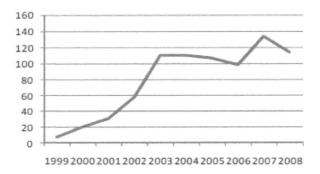

Figure 11:   Cases of consolidation into 100% subsidiary

Source: Recof MARR Statistics.

This trend which is also shown in Figure 11 based on statistics by Recof, reflects the fact that there are situations that make a balanced control impractical. This may be because many parent companies need to take a leading role in restructuring businesses and in centralizing strategic decision making. Kikutani and Saito (2006) commented that this phenomenon is particularly interesting because many parent companies already have ownership in excess of 50%, but yet pursue to yield full ownership. The implication of removing minority shareholders to gain freedom over the control of a subsidiary, is that firstly, where there are strong synergies between the parent's and subsidiary's businesses, there is a strong incentive for the parent company to have full control over the subsidiary. This is consistent with the complementarity of assets view discussed in Section 4.2. Secondly, where there are overlapping business activities, the parent may want to take the leading role in restructuring those activities so as to improve the group's overall efficiency. And thirdly, there may be conflict of interests over the distribution of a residual profit, such as when a parent company wants to withhold distribution of residual profit to the minority shareholders, and use the retained earnings instead to reinvest in growth.

5.3 VERTICAL AND HORIZONTAL COORDINATION

This section looks at the coordination systems that corporations use to manage subsidiaries. A theory that depicts well Japanese group management practices can be found in the Owan and Kato (2011) model that compares three information processing systems: vertical, horizontal and hybrid. According to their model, there are two types of information that affect the choice of optimal actions. First, there is systematic environmental information that affects the optimal action in each task systematically. For example, macro-economic conditions, emergence of new technology and changes in customer taste. Then there is also local environmental information that is observed only by those working on each task. Adaptation calls for the use of local information, and firms choose their information processing system that minimizes their total costs.

In what they described as a vertical control system, decision rights are retained in the hands of the management to coordinate perfectly among tasks at the expense of adaptation. When systematic information possessed at the top is sufficient to infer precisely the local information collected at the lower levels of organization, management will try to pre-specify both primary and complementary actions to minimize coordination losses. But then management's instructions may not always be understood correctly by their employees. There could be communication errors, distortion, or delay in implementation, during which the environment may have changed. Workers may not use their discretion because they may not have adequate knowledge, and thus may not be capable of figuring out how they can improve upon the instructions of management. However, if workers can have full understanding of the production technology, they would then be capable of adjusting the management's instructions whilst using the local information they perfectly observe, even within a hierarchical vertical control system. Such an arrangement is what Owan and Kato describe as the hybrid type coordination.

In the case of a horizontal coordination system, tasks are bundled and delegated to teams such as subsidiaries to enhance the capability for adaptation and achieve perfect coordination within teams. A firm exercising horizontal coordination would have to consider in advance the probability that its workers will perfectly understand and take complementary action, and then optimally choose the degree of task bundling, multitasking and investment in communication quality.

This judgement could be based on given existing conditions of the firm such as the capability of training its employees, the firm's labour management relations, corporate culture, and quality of work force. Some firms I have talked to deliberately allow departments or subsidiaries to overlap their functions so as to generate shared knowledge. This obviously comes with a cost, and the management in trying to minimize this cost function, will use teamwork and communication channels only when it is worth doing so. In other words, horizontal coordination becomes viable only when the importance of adaptation exceeds a certain threshold. Delegating strategically or operationally critical decisions to lower-level employees is very unlikely when adaptation is less critical because the horizontal coordination system typically requires substantial investment in employee training and is not worth doing unless the adaptation effort generates sufficient return.

As technological and market changes become ever more disruptive in today's world, it would appear that primary actions and coordination responsibilities are less likely to be delegated to lower-level employees, because local information is less likely to be sufficient for the employees to engage in complex coordination activities. Systematic information may become more important and labour-management communication involve less noise, such that a vertical control system may become more desirable. But on the other hand, if adaptation to new environment becomes more important, and if the pre-conditions that facilitate team communication improve, allowing investment to become more viable, then horizontal coordination may become more desirable.

Following this theory, it appears then that whether or not to invest in integrating subsidiaries into important decision making would depend on the level of returns such an adaptation would likely generate. But as we shall see later in the case study chapter, though it is still arguable that the investment decision is highly dependent on the role and importance of the subsidiary concerned, Japanese corporate groups do have hybrid systems that allow for both vertical and horizontal coordination. Although hierarchical structures are often perceived to be incompatible with delegation or team organizations, firms seem to try to combine the empowerment approach with the traditional hierarchical structure. In hybrid organizations, employees adjust their actions according to local information, after receiving instructions from management.

In a hybrid coordination system, workers adjust the management's instructions using the local information they perfectly observe. Adaptation and coordination losses are smaller in the hybrid coordination system than in the vertical control system because local information is utilized in the hybrid. However, the rationality required for employees in hybrid coordination system is higher than that required for those in the vertical control system. In the vertical system, employees only need to execute what is prescribed by management. In the hybrid system, employees have to predict what complementary actions their colleagues might choose and solve the cost minimization problem. Therefore, only firms with capable employees and complementary practices can implement the hybrid coordination system. In a parent and subsidiary setting, often experts seconded from the parent company to the subsidiary company, or vice versa, act as facilitators that coordinate vertically and horizontally.

The hybrid coordination system described above relates to what Aoki (2010) describes as "reciprocal essentialities", which is a generic mode of organizational architecture where management and workers cannot increase their marginal products in the absence of the other's cooperation. Aoki presented four other generic modes, and posited that the extent to which either or both management and workers are essential can condition their relative bargaining power and hence their incentives to invest in their specific skills, If only one of them is essential, then the holder of those assets can gain bargaining power even without the cooperation of the other. And if task environments are different, then cognitive sharing may not be worth the communication costs because the information is relatively unrelated. This idea of essentiality can likewise be applied to parent–subsidiary relationship and to the coordination of activities within a corporate group. Similarly, the kind of overall knowledge required in coordination is also described in Tregaski's (2010) case study of InksCo (a printing-inks business belonging to the chemical division of an oil company),

"To control the product modification process any process changes had to be authorized centrally as only InksCo was seen as having the overarching knowledge about the product's capability. ... Equally it was seen as InksCo's role to access the necessary country-specific product knowledge [from other subsidiaries] to ensure the effective functioning of global products."

Tregaski's case study on the strategic role of subsidiaries highlights the importance of vertical and horizontal coordination and the capability of doing so. As I will discuss later in the case studies, many Japanese companies exhibit having such horizontal and vertical coordination systems that are used alongside the delegation of decision rights to subsidiaries.

5.4 MONITORING OF SUBSIDIARIES

Although subsidiaries are independent legal entities, Company Law and consolidated financial reporting in Japan deems it necessary for parent companies to monitor their subsidiaries and be aware of activities that may have substantial impact on the corporate group. Shareholders may regard a failure in governance as a breach of duty of diligence by the board members, and legal charges may be brought against them or directly against the board members of the subsidiary concerned. Governance includes internal control systems such as proper delegation of decision rights, vertical and horizontal coordination systems, performance management systems, as well as accounting and internal auditing.

The level of monitoring may depend on many factors such as the bargaining power between the parent and its subsidiary. According to the results of an analysis of over 500 samples performed by Ito, Kikutani and Hayashida (2003), monitoring of subsidiary tends to increase as the bargaining power of the parent company increases, and decreases as the subsidiary's bargaining power increases. Their bargaining power depends on factors such as equity ownership, amount of transaction, dependency on finance, and amount of procurement. The result is consistent with the theoretical expectation that subsidiaries that trade extensively with entities outside the corporate group are disciplined by the external market, thereby reducing the need and incentive for the parent to monitor it so long as there is no conflict of interest, and the subsidiary continues to invest in firm specific assets that are required by the parent company. Governance and monitoring are not seen as uniform across all parent–subsidiary relationships, but as contingent upon their bargain power and the factors that affect them.

Although their analysis did not distinguish between different types of parent–subsidiary relationship as Ito *et al.* did, their findings show that:

- There is negative correlation between size of subsidiary and frequency of BS/PL monitoring.
- There is positive correlation between size of subsidiary and strength of *ex-post* monitoring.
- Complementary relation between delegation of strategic decision making and monitoring (measured by frequency and strength) cannot be identified in governance of subsidiaries, thus indicating possibility of moral hazard and governance problems.

Despite a growing number of firms forming corporate groups and delegating activities to subsidiaries, there appears to be insufficient performance monitoring by parent companies. An empirical study by Miyajima and Aoki's (2010) analyzed the issue of dual agency, meaning agency problems that exist both between shareholder and top management, and also between top management and its business units and subsidiaries, and remarked that in light of the diverse and complicated business portfolio many corporate groups have today, the risks of severe information asymmetries, communication problems and dysfunctional strategic decision making have become much higher. In addition to conventional principal agent problems, there exists another layer of agency problems between top management and its business units and subsidiaries that needs to be addressed. Their empirical findings show that the issue of dual agency is worrisome because the increase of delegation to subsidiaries has not been accompanied with an increase in monitoring (measured by instances of periodical performance monitoring), which should be implemented to complement delegation.

Figure 12: Percentage of sample firms that conduct internal auditing on subsidiary and related companies

Source: Journal of the Institute of Internal Auditors Japan No. 6, 2011.

But whether monitoring is insufficient may depend on how it is measured. If we measure by coverage of internal auditing rather than by instances of performance monitoring, results may appear different. Figure 12 based on the Institute of Internal Auditors Japan's survey data, shows a rise in the percentage of firms that conduct internal auditing on subsidiary and related companies.

Owing to the enforced legal responsibility of corporate board members to ensure appropriateness of activities within the corporate group, firms today are placing more emphasis on subsidiaries in their internal auditing. Poor performance of a subsidiary can affect the share price of the parent company, and misconduct by a subsidiary can bring reputational damage to the entire group. And in either case, shareholders may bring charges against the management for negligence.

5.5 MANAGING TENSION BETWEEN PARENT AND SUBSIDIARY

Managing conflict and tension between parent and subsidiary is another important activity, not necessarily because conflicts are harmful, but because conflicts could bring positive consequences such as innovation, change and improvements. Blazejewski and Becker-Ritterspach (2011)

gave a concise overview of the various different theoretical lenses that could be applied to headquarters–subsidiary conflict including the following:

(1) Contingency theory

   Firms face pressures for differentiation such as local responsiveness, and pressures for integration. The challenge is to find the right balance and trade-off in decision making while maintaining the balance between the two forces. Amongst the range of tools that can be used to manage conflicting pressures, emphasis was placed on the coordination mechanism of normative integration through socialization, in which managerial mind-sets are integrated. Managers need to be socialized in such a way that shared understandings of the corporate group's broader purpose and goals are achieved.

(2) Agency theory

   Agency problems arise when agents take advantage of information asymmetries and pursue interests that diverge from the principal's goals. Agency problems can be reduced by applying monitoring systems and by designing contracts that are incentive compatible. Conflict also arises because headquarters and subsidiaries hold diverging information and perceptions about each other's level of competencies. Conflict generation can be countered by implementing context enhancing mechanisms such as frequent information meetings.

(3) Game theory

   There are various types of games, and the mixed motive games corresponds well to the situation of subsidiaries and headquarters, where subsidiaries pursue local interests while at the same time share an interest in the corporate group's overall prosperity and survival. The dynamics of players having different goals are introduced through repeated games. Evolutionary game theory, which will be discussed in a later section, allows players to change their strategy over time, taking into account contextual embedded-ness of conflict process.

(4) Institutionalism

In the process of knowledge transfer, if a practice is perceived by the employees at a recipient unit to be in conflict with the regulatory, cognitive and normative institutions of the host context, the implementation and internalization will be difficult. Institutional distance and institutional duality define the crucial causes of conflict pressures.

(5) Micro-politics

There is the view that institutional diversity is the root cause of conflicts, and the view that actors have the ability to follow interests that are not simply reflective of macro-societal embeddedness, that things like personal career outlook and idiosyncratic interests determine the outcomes of conflict. There is also the view that institutions set constraints within which political activity within firms can operate, shaping the preference of actors and the feasibility of certain courses of action, but they do not determine outcomes on their own.

The above theoretical perspectives are related to goal incompatibility, where practices, knowledge and tasks of the head-office are incompatible with the goals of the subsidiary. Along this line of literature, Geppert and Dorrenbacher (2011) described how multinational companies (MNCs) must comply with the different institutionalized expectations of the various institutional environments in which they operate. They discussed two conflicting isomorphic pulls. First there is the international pull of the overall strategies and structures of the MNC. Then there is also the national pull of expectations within local host countries. External institutional pulls lead to tensions based on diverse institutional pressures, while internal isomorphic pulls leads to convergence and adoption of similar organizational strategies and structures across the corporate group. Conflicting isomorphic pulls are especially a problem when institutional distance between home country of an MNC, where the organizational practice originates, and the host country, where the practices are transferred, is high, resulting in a situation where institutional pressures such as regulative mechanisms, normative mechanisms, and cognitive-cultural mechanisms are very different for the parent company than they are for the subsidiary.

There are other conflict related issues such as the dilemma of deciding how much power needs to be centralized at the headquarter level, and how much power needs to be shared with subsidiaries in order to be able to effectively manage operations. As these decisions are highly influenced by how the parent company understands the capabilities of its subsidiaries, perception gap that is often caused by communication problems could have serious consequences. Hence identifying perception gaps might be the most critical coordination task involved in improving and sustaining overall performance of a corporate group. Schmid and Daniel (2011) pointed out that while perception gaps between the headquarters and the subsidiary concerning the subsidiary's role can generate conflict, the issue on role perception has been largely neglected in international business literature. They discussed theoretical developments such as the role theory, which can be applied to understand subsidiary roles as patterns of behaviour that are related to a specific position in the corporate group and that fulfil a particular function for the corporate group. The subsidiary and members of the role set may have different perceptions of the subsidiary's role and consequently differing expectations regarding the related role behaviour. For example, a subsidiary may overestimate its own capabilities in a certain area, or the parent company may be unaware of and, therefore, underestimate the subsidiary's capabilities. This implies that if there are important perception gaps regarding subsidiary roles, behaviour of members in the role set will not mesh and cooperative action may be difficult to achieve. Although perception gap is very much a cognitive concept, perceptions are central triggers of action.

In the next chapter, based on my case study findings, we will look at how Japanese corporate groups use coordination mechanisms, such as assigning a counter-part department in the head-office for each subsidiary, to identify or minimize perception gaps as well as to manage conflict.

5.6 NORMS AND SELF-ENFORCING GOVERNANCE

In addition to having some form of control, a parent company also needs to depend on the subsidiary's self-enforcing governance. From a new institutional economics approach, North (1992) wrote that we have incomplete information and limited capacity by which to process information. Institutions, defined as rules of the game consisting formal rules and informal social norms that govern individual behaviour, are, therefore, formed to reduce uncertainty in human exchange. So institutions matter when transactions become costlier. North stressed that successful developmental policy entails an understanding of the dynamics of economic change if policies pursued are to have desired consequences. Similarly, Ostrom (2011) illustrated how the Institutional Analysis and Developmental Framework can be applied to analyze all types of institutional arrangements, including parent and subsidiary transactions. A key part of the framework is the identification of an action situation and the resulting patterns of interactions and outcomes, and evaluating those outcomes, with the potential to reform them. For example, within the framework of an action situation is a set of actors. Assuming them to be *homo economicus* would be unrealistic, and, therefore, one could alternatively assume that individuals are unreliable learners, and also that the various institutional arrangements offer the actors different incentives and opportunities to learn. When such individuals interact in frequently repeated and simple situations, it is possible to model them as if they had complete information.

In predicting outcomes within an action situation, we may assume that in many situations, individuals, instead of making completely independent decisions, may be socially embedded such that initial norms and fairness may change the outcome of the situation. The individuals may also change their strategies over time as they learn about results of past actions. The predicted outcomes as well as other likely outcomes and trade-offs that could be achieved under alternative institutional arrangements may then be evaluated.

Action situations can be viewed as partially dependent on rules, and institutional analysis first attempts to understand the working rules and norms that individuals use in making decisions. For example, one can be interested in rule configuration and in how the stability of formal rule-ordered actions is dependent on the shared meaning assigned to words used to formulate the rules. If no shared meaning exists (such as regarding the role of a subsidiary), or if the meanings (such as role expectation of a subsidiary) are changed, there may be confusion about actions required. Or one can be interested in how informal rules such as shared value systems affect the ways individuals organize their relationship with one another. Many rules in use are not written down by participants as rules, and there are also settings where rules have evolved over long periods of time and are understood implicitly by old participants but not new comers.

Aoki (2001) focused on the issue of enforceability, and questioned when the rules of the game become enforceable. Aoki posited that rules of the game are endogenously generated, and thus become self-enforcing through the strategic interactions of the agents including the enforcer of the rules. The basic issue is to understand the complexity of institutional arrangements as an instance of multiple equilibria of some kind, and to understand the mechanism of institutional change in a framework consistent with the equilibrium view of institutions. Aoki uses what he calls a comparative institutional Analysis to understand why particular institutional arrangements have evolved in one economy but not in others.

Looking at earlier game theory perspectives, Hurwicz (1993) has formalized the notion of enforceability in terms of Nash equilibrium where no player has the incentive to change his strategy. In order for a set of humanly devised rules to be enforceable, it is said that it must contain a Nash equilibrium. The concern is to inquire the possibility of designing an institution which can implement a given social goal in a way that is compatible with the incentives of the players. If the mechanism is not self-enforceable, then it needs to be supplemented by an enforcement mechanism. Within this equilibrium-of-the-game notion of institution, the repeated game approach attempts to understand mechanisms that enable institutions to remain stable. The underlying condition is that an economically rational player selects his strategy whilst acknowledging his relationship of mutual dependency with other players. Although this approach captures the aspect of self-enforceability of institutions, it does not explain the process of what forms the institution or how multiple equilibria are being converged to one equilibrium. Therefore, as Abe and Kawakami (2010) described, the evolutionary game approach is better suited to address these issues.

Aoki (2010), in considering the self-governing question, argued that different modes of corporate associational (group-level) cognition call for different forms of governance in order to satisfy the fundamental requirement of self-governance. Aoki posited that if cognitions organized within an organization in some systematic way, then reasonable coherent decisions may be made for collective action, and that to facilitate and exploit this possibility is one of the most important *raison d'être* of a corporation. By intentional design as well as through conventions and routines that evolve during overlapping generations of its members, cognitions are systematically distributed among managers and workers. Although agency problems cannot be completely controlled, Aoki posited that organizational mode is not selected primarily in order to control opportunistic behaviour, but rather to benefit from working together.

Aoki proposed that at the societal level, the strategies of individuals and organizations together shape the process of co-evolution. Given an evolutionary outcome of this outcome at the societal level, the general rules (understanding) lead to the concept of the organizational field where corporate organizations of a similar mode cluster and compete. With such rules as a basic referential frame, individuals then form their own cognitive frames of organizational games that they play. It is such shared general understanding that essentially makes business corporations self-governing. Although individual cognitive frames are different from one another in specific level, within a particular organization, these frames meet together and generate a common frame for team-play.

Of societal rules and norms, Aoki added that although rules may be seen as constraining because ignoring them will not be beneficial, they are also enabling because rules can aid individual's knowledge of how others are likely to play, thus helping them to play effectively by providing prescriptions for effective action choices. Once a norm is established, each member no longer needs to calculate prescribed strategies from scratch. The norm provides a cognitive frame for the members to which they can offload their cognitive burden. For example, in a workplace, the culture of setting individual work target was generated by the workers themselves, but once established it was experienced as a set of externally imposed shop floor norms.

Having briefly reviewed ways in which norms could be established, we will later in the case studies see how norms can help parent and subsidiary use their shared knowledge to coordinate activities effectively.

5.7 DIFFUSION OF KNOWLEDGE

We now look at another aspect of managing subsidiaries, that of the diffusion of knowledge, rules, and best practices. This diffusion can flow from both directions, from the parent to the subsidiary, as well as from the subsidiary to the parent, and we shall look at each of these individually.

5.7.1 Diffusion of Knowledge from Parent to Subsidiary

A subsidiary may adopt certain managerial ideas and best practices not necessarily because they are seen as efficient, but because adoption is seen as crucial in order to enhance the subsidiary's legitimacy. Dual institutional pressures often play an important role in defining various degrees of adoption of organizational practices. According to Geppert and Dorrenbacher (2011), in the case of MNCs, the degree of social and societal embedded-ness differs significantly between capital societies. Best practices, therefore, need to be adapted locally when transferred to other countries. This is also because transferring of management practices from one context to another is not simply a matter of moving knowledge, but a generative process of producing new knowledge and new ways of knowing by engaging in the activity of performance management in the new context (Fenton-O'Creevy, Gooderham and Cerdin, 2011). In other words, expertise requires extensive participation in practice, and the social institutions in which we partake frame the ways we know.

For example, a senior manager who discusses issues with other senior managers across functions is tied into a web of cognitive activity, making him part of a thinking system within the company. His expertise, therefore, lies in his ability to access and engage with the intellectual resources of the community in which he is part of. This explains why some star performers succeed in one company but fail when transferred to another company, where he is incapable of accessing and mobilizing knowledge. If knowledge transfer is dependent on exposure to collective knowledge, it then implies that without such exposure, as in the case of parent and subsidiary interaction, cognitive hurdles will prevent knowledge transfer. It also implies that concerned parties must be motivated to be engaged in exposure processes.

The social embedded-ness in the local host country may constitute a serious challenge to the head-quarter's monopoly over strategy. This local embedded-ness may also result in knowledge that is so highly integrated in the local context that transfer is not readily achievable even in the absence of political resistance. Fenton-O'Creevy, Gooderham and Cerdin (2011) posited that a transfer of knowledge-based practices across MNCs confronts both micro-political resistance and local cognitive hurdles, and that overcoming them depends on whether there are skilled actors who possess bridging social capital. They presented four possible outcomes of knowledge transfer attempts as shown in Figure 13, and argued that where there is considerable exposure to shared cognitive social processes and shared goals, transfer of knowledge could be achieved with little customization. However, when significant local customization is required, knowledge may be reconstructed and translated into local context, yet remain consistent with the original purpose of the transfer. For example, where local customization is required, many Japanese firms rearrange their *Omotenashi* or Japanese style service to suit local needs. They also contended that a lack of exposure to shared cognitive social processes or the absence of shared goals may lead to low internalization, and thus result in ceremonial adoption or corruption of the intended knowledge transfer.

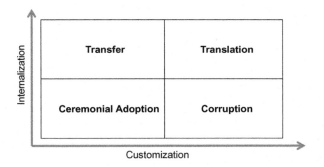

Figure 13: Four possible outcomes of knowledge transfer
Source: Fenton-O'Creevy, Gooderham and Cerdin (2011) p. 107, Fig. 4.2.

Conflict can bring about dysfunctional outcomes. Schotter and Beamish (2011) described dysfunctional conflict behaviours that subsidiaries could exhibit. Subsidiaries could ignore the headquarter initiative, though they could not do so indefinitely. Or subsidiaries could use distraction tactics to avoid implementation, leading to otherwise unnecessary efforts and inefficiency. Subsidiaries could also obstruct or attack the headquarter initiatives, and create intense relational conflict.

One way of handling dual pressures and conflict is to have individual agents with multiple social community memberships within a corporate group to bridge structural holes in social networks and the transfer of knowledge. Such agents are then able to bring knowledge and ways of thinking from one domain into another, thus contributing to the emergence of new ideas. On the other hand, this also implies that corporate groups that lack such bridging agents may experience considerable difficulty in integrating and brokering collective knowledge. The use of secondments and transfers of managers from the parent company to the subsidiary may well be for this purpose of creating such multiple memberships.

5.7.2 Diffusion of Knowledge from Subsidiary to Group

Having looked at diffusion of knowledge from parent to subsidiary, we now look at the flow of knowledge from subsidiary to group. In many international business literatures on MNCs, the role of subsidiaries has been reduced to adaptation of centrally set strategies. Although focus has been on helping MNC management to overcome strategic and structural misfits in responding to external environmental pressures, subsidiaries can themselves be active participants in the formulation and implementation of corporate strategy.

Birkinshaw *et al.* (1998) showed in their research that subsidiaries play an increasingly important role as contributors to the development of firm-specific advantages. Birkinshaw argued that firms that engage in overseas production must have some form of proprietary advantage to compensate for the natural disadvantage of competing with established firms in a foreign land. While some of these advantages or resources are location bound, others are not, and they can, therefore, be leveraged by the corporate group in other regions. In other words, these resources have the potential to contribute to the MNC's firm specific advantage.

But these resources need to be discovered and recognized by the corporate management otherwise they will remain resources of limited used within the local region. Recognition can be a top-down process where the corporate headquarter identifies the subsidiary's competencies through communication. Or the process can be a bottom-up one where entrepreneurial efforts by the subsidiary demonstrate their capability and willingness to take on responsibilities. Birkinshaw defines the subsidiary's contributory role as the extent to which the subsidiary has specialized resources that are recognized by the corporation as a whole. This implies that by defining an appropriate structural context, corporate management can either promote or inhibit the development of the subsidiary's contributory role.

In other words, having specialized resources are not sufficient in themselves. Subsidiary initiative and entrepreneurship are needed to make the resources known to the corporate headquarter and thereby gain recognition. Communication and certain amount of autonomy are also necessary to empower and encourage the subsidiary to utilize those resources more effectively within the corporate group. Whether the benefits are sufficient to counterbalance the dangers of control loss and opportunism is a separate question. The point here is that the subsidiary's initiative as well as the ability of the corporate system to effectively leverage subsidiary resources, can potentially make the subsidiary's resources part of the firm's specific advantage.

Subsidiary that has knowledge that is perceived as critical and scarce can use that knowledge as a power resource. Tregaskis (2003) showed that subsidiaries that have greater autonomy and overall responsibility over product development are more likely to encourage inter-organizational learning networks because external knowledge is often critical in the renewal of knowledge, especially where the organization has limited access to relevant skills and knowledge. The widespread adoption of the subsidiary's knowledge also signals the legitimacy of the knowledge and helps reinforce the subsidiary's strategic role. External knowledge, therefore, can act as a source of power when it provides the organization with capabilities it cannot generate internally.

Whitley, Morgan, Kelly and Sharpe (2003) suggested that the weak domestic economy in Japan has made foreign operations more important as possible sources of markets and profits. As Japanese MNCs begin to produce a significant proportion of their outputs abroad, they should consider changing their focus from merely transferring and applying domestic recipes to adapting and learning from local innovations. The extent of change, however, is likely to vary considerably between firms in different sectors.

In their case study of financial firms, they showed that learning from foreign operations was not a high priority for Japanese banks in the 1980s. The use of expatriate managers to acquire international "specialist" knowledge in international capital markets was restricted because it was in conflict with established "generalist" career patterns. "To be posted abroad was a sign of inferior status since all important decisions and developments were made in Tokyo and Osaka ... To be an international banker was to be regarded as a specialist in an organization that valued generalist skills." This was also because domestic clients and markets continue to be the dominant source of revenue. Partly because of the highly centralized decision making that delayed major transactions, Japanese banks often suffered losses from lending to foreign borrowers, and this reinforced their preference for dealing with domestic clients. In the post bubble period of the 1990s, this pattern was evident in banks that reacted by concentrating recovery plans on serving Japanese customers. But some financial firms in the study took a more positive approach and saw the role of expatriates as one of learning and transferring new techniques from London and New York to Tokyo. This may be because of the growing recognition accorded to specialist technical skills in international banking, such that becoming a specialist became an increasingly attractive option. Developments appeared to have gone furthest in large security firms, where the balance of business had shifted from Japanese corporate client oriented towards deal making in European capital markets.

In another case study by Whitley, Morgan, Kelly and Sharpe (2003) on car manufacturing companies, they identified three distinct stages in which the role of expatriate managers in overseas subsidiaries changes. During the initial phase of building plants, there was considerable reliance on Japanese managers and engineers, but after the plant was built and operations were running well, the number of Japanese managers declined and their roles became more advisory. Most senior management posts were given to local staffs. In the third stage, which only few firms had reached, the number of expatriates was further reduced, and their role was seen as being more supportive than directive. The prevalent impression was "a rather ad hoc process of selection and assignment of expatriate managers, and limited attempts to learn systematically from their experiences when they went back to Japan." Senior managers in Japan were reluctant to cede much authority to regional units, and functional reporting to divisional head offices in Japan remains dominant. These case study findings are consistent with the empirical research finding of Kaiho (1999), which shows a low degree of power delegation to overseas subsidiaries. Whitley *et al.* concluded that on the whole, managerial careers remain relatively generalist, and this is not likely to change if firm-specific way of managing continues to be regarded as crucial to success in all markets. But while internationalization remains based on domestic recipes, there are cases where the actual production layout is being continuously updated and modified by Japanese managers such that every new plant is different from the previous plant.

In this section, we have reviewed some major literatures on how knowledge is diffused to subsidiaries and how, although often overlooked, subsidiaries too can contribute in disseminating best practices to the parent or other members of the corporate group. Later in the case study, we will look at the case where an IT subsidiary has managed to share best practices with its parent company. This section also highlighted the importance of brokering collective knowledge by agents, who can mediate from both the parent and the subsidiary's perspectives.

Chapter 6

CASE STUDY: BRIDGING THEORY AND PRACTICE

6.1 METHODOLOGY

Having discussed several main theories and literatures regarding corporate groups in Chapters 4 and 5, this chapter aims to bring together theory and practice by looking at how academic knowledge matches with real world situations that Japanese corporate groups face. The following key management aspects of corporate group management will be discussed: (a) Decision regarding boundary of the corporate group, (b) Vertical and horizontal coordination of subsidiaries, (c) Delegation of decision rights, and (d) Self-enforcing mechanisms.

Regarding methodology, I have chosen to use case studies for the following reasons. Firstly, although there are literatures on various aspects of corporate group management, there appears to be very little case studies on Japanese corporate groups that show how companies actually manage their subsidiaries. Findings from cases can be used to expand existing theories or fill gaps that have not hitherto been addressed. Secondly, because the research questions are essentially how and why questions, following the design and methods for case study research proposed by Yin (2009), the explanatory nature of this research work prompts the use of cases as a preferable method. Thirdly, this research on why firms form groups and how firms manage groups does not require control of behavioural events and experiments. And finally, the distinct advantage of using cases is that it allows me to investigate the contemporary phenomenon of corporate groups in depth and within its real-world context. It also allows me to deal with a full variety of evidence, from documents and archival data to interviews and observations.

For the purpose of conducting an in-depth analysis, I have selected five corporate groups — three from the manufacturing industry and two from the transportation industry. The three manufacturing corporations are Hitachi, Panasonic, and Mitsubishi Heavy Industry, and the two transportation corporations are Nihon Yusen and Japan Airlines. These cases represent fairly well large corporate groups in Japan, though I must also admit there were several other firms I had originally intended to interview but could not to obtain their consent. Nonetheless, the in-depth study of the above mentioned five corporate groups sufficiently satisfies the purpose of this book. The cases are not meant to be used for producing any statistical generalizations of populations or universes. Rather the purpose is to provide an analytic generalization on how large corporations manage their subsidiaries. In other words, replication of findings in the cases and not sampling logic substantiates the induction that is proposed in this work.

Information on the above mentioned corporate groups were gathered based on interviews conducted between September 2012 and January 2013, and numerous follow-up communications to clarify certain facts there have been missed out in the interviews. In order for the interviews to be conducted efficiently, a common list of 15 questions concerning reasons for establishing subsidiaries, classification and role of subsidiaries, control and coordination of subsidiaries, parent–subsidiary relationship and conflict, and competence development was sent in advance to the companies. This allowed time for the companies to assign appropriate persons and to think over the interview questions. Questions were phrased carefully so as to not to influence the respondent's answers. They were thus neither too narrow such that they would insinuate desired answers, nor were they too broad such that they would be ineffective in eliciting information that suffices the purpose of the interviews. All the persons who were interviewed were head-office managers responsible for supervising and coordinating subsidiaries. After each interview, a case report was written to document information that was collected. Securities Report (*Yukashouken Houkokusho*) from 2007 to 2011, IR releases, publicly available information and new sources were also collected and used to supplement the cases.

6.2 AN OVERVIEW OF FIVE CORPORATE GROUPS AND THEIR SUBSIDIARIES

This section describes briefly the following five corporate groups that have been chosen for the case study: Hitachi Group, Panasonic Group, Mitsubishi Heavy Industry Group, Nihon Yusen Group and Japan Airlines Group.

Hitachi Group

Hitachi, which began as a machines repair factory in 1910, was established as a company in 1920 by its founder Namihei Odaira. With harmony, sincerity, and frontier spirit as its founding spirit, Hitachi's corporate philosophy was to contribute to the society through developing its own technology and products of excellent quality. Over its 100 years of history, Hitachi has been a major leading innovation company in Japan. Being the first to manufacture electric train in 1924, electric refrigerator in 1932, and nuclear power plant in 1974, Hitachi has also been renowned for its many other contributions such as railway seat reservations system in 1959, super computer S-810 in 1982, the 300 series bullet train in 1993. As of 31st March 2014, Hitachi, which consists of 947 consolidated subsidiary companies and 231 related companies, has ten reported business segments, including information and communication systems, electric power systems, social industrial systems, electronic equipment, construction machinery, high-functional material, automotive systems, digital media and home appliances, financial service and others. Its diverse range of activities includes product development, manufacturing, sales and services.

Panasonic Group

Founded by Konosuke Matsushita in 1918, Panasonic (known prior to 2008 as Matsushita Electric Industrial) is a household name for home appliance products. As of 31st March 2014, Panasonic, which consists of 504 consolidated subsidiaries, has five reported business segments, including AVC networks, appliance, eco solutions, automotive & industrial systems, and others. According to the Nikkei 2012 Industry Map, Panasonic has top domestic market share in products such as washing machine, car navigation, room air conditioner, IH cooking heater, blue ray disc player, and lithium-ion battery.

Mitsubishi Heavy Industry Group

The roots of Mitsubishi Heavy Industry (MHI) can be traced to the founding of what was to become Mitsubishi in 1870 by Yataro Iwasaki. The early ship building business expanded into other heavy industry businesses, such that by 1934, MHI has established its position as the largest private firm in Japan, manufacturing ships, heavy machinery, airplanes and railroad cars. Today (as of 31st March 2014), MHI, which consists 290 consolidated subsidiaries and 39 related companies, has five reported business segments, including energy and environment, commercial aviation and transportation systems, integrated defence & space systems, machinery equipment and infrastructure, and others.

Nihon Yusen Group

Founded in 1885, the Nihon Yusen (NYK) Group is a comprehensive global logistics enterprise that offers ocean, land and air transport services. As of 31st March 2014, Nihon Yusen, which consists of 610 consolidated subsidiaries and 130 related companies which, has seven reported business segments, including liner, air cargo transportation, logistics, bulk and specialized carriers, cruise ship services, real estate and others. NYK aims to leverage its logistics and technological capabilities to effectively capture Asia's growing transportation and supply chain needs. According to the Nikkei Industry Map, NYK liners have transported 372,440 TEUs in 2010, accounting to 3% of global market share.

Japan Airlines Group

Established in 1951, Japan Airlines is one of Japan's major network airlines, and has services including code-sharing (as of 1st April 2014) on 363 international routes and 128 domestic routes, covering 280 airports in 45 countries and regions. Although the company filed for reorganization proceedings in January 2010, the proceedings were completed in March of the following year. After massive restructuring, which were guided by Japan's management guru, Kazuo Inamori, the company re-emerged as a much healthier company, yielding double digit operating profit margins now for two consecutive years. As of 31st March 2014, Japan Airlines consisted of 95 consolidated subsidiaries and 59 related companies.

All five corporate groups have head-office departments for each core business unit, and each core business unit has subsidiaries that perform activities for that business unit. Tables 8 and 9 show the roles of some of the major subsidiaries in the five corporate groups.

Hitachi and Panasonic use what is called the *company system* to manage their diversified business units and subsidiaries. Although called a "company", it is not a separate legal entity, but essentially a large business division within the corporate group that has a high degree of autonomy and which bears responsibility over profit and losses of the businesses that it operates.

From Tables 8 and 9, we can see these major subsidiaries in the five corporate groups are involved in a wide array of activities. Some subsidiaries are responsible for multiple vertically integrated functions ranging from manufacturing to sales and after-service. Some subsidiaries, however, specialize only in narrow up-stream activities such as product design and manufacturing, or down-stream activities such as logistics and sales within its business value chain. Some have transactions mainly with the parent company and contribute to the corporate group as cost centres, while some operate independent businesses and contribute as profit centres.

Although the tables cover only a small portion of the vast number of subsidiaries the groups in the five case studies have, we can roughly see the roles major subsidiaries have within the corporate value chain, and we can infer from this broad picture that there has to be some form of control and coordination systems that enable these large corporate groups to coordinate masses of decisions and activities whilst executing their corporate strategies. In the following

Table 8: Three corporate groups in the manufacturing industry and their subsidiaries

	BU Divisions	Subsidiaries (Manufacturing)	Subsidiaries (Sales & Services)
Hitachi	**In-House Companies** ① Power Systems Company ② Infrastructure Systems Company ③ Rail Systems Company ④ Urban Planning and Development Systems Company ⑤ Defense Systems Company ⑥ Information & Telecommunication Systems Company **Business Divisions** ⑦ Semiconductor Business Division ⑧ Consumer Business Division ⑨ Automotive Systems Business Management Division	① Babcock Hitachi, GE Hitachi Nuclear Energy ② Hitachi Industrial Equipment Systems, Hitachi Elevator (China) ④ Hitachi Construction ⑥ Hitachi Omron Terminal Solutions, Hitachi Computer Products (America), Hitachi Computer Products Europe ⑦ Hitachi High-Technologies, Hitachi Koki, Hitachi Kokusai Electric, Hitachi Via Mechanics ⑧ Hitachi Appliances, Hitachi Consumer Electronics, Hitachi Consumer Products (Thailand) ⑨ Hitachi Automotive Systems, Clarion	① Hitachi Engineering and Service, Hitachi Power Europe, Hitachi Power Systems America ② Hitachi Building Systems, Hitachi Plant Technologies ③ Hitachi Rail Europe ⑥ Hitachi Information & Control Solutions, Hitachi Solutions, Hitachi Systems, Hitachi Consulting, Hitachi Data Systems, Hitachi Information & Telecommunication Systems Global Holding ⑧ Hitachi LG Data Storage **Others** Hitachi Transport System
Panasonic	**In-House Companies** -Consumer Products- ① AVC Network Company ② Appliances Company -Solutions- ③ Systems & Communications Company ④ Eco Solutions Company ⑤ Healthcare Company ⑥ Manufacturing Solutions Company -Devices- ⑦ Automotive Systems Company ⑧ Industrial Devices Company ⑨ Energy Company	① Panasonic Liquid Crystal Display, Panasonic Plasma Display, Panasonic North America, Panasonic Avionics ② Sanyo Electric, Panasonic AP Air Conditioning (Guangzhou) ③ Panasonic System Networks, Panasonic Mobile Communications ④ Panasonic Eco Systems, Panasonic Lighting Europe ⑤ Panasonic Healthcare ⑥ Panasonic Factory Solutions ⑦ Panasonic Automotive Systems Dalian ⑧ Panasonic Electronic Devices, Panasonic Semiconductor Asia ⑨ Sanyo Electric, Sanyo Energy (Suzhou)	Panasonic Consumer Marketing, Panasonic North America, Panasonic Marketing Europe, Panasonic Asia-Pacific, Panasonic China

Mitsubishi Heavy Industries	Divisions		
	① Shipbuilding & Ocean Development	① MHI Maritech, Choryo Senpaku Koji	① MHI Engineering, Kanmon Dock Service
	② Power Systems	②③ Choryo Sekkei, MHI Precision Casting, Mitsubishi FBR Systems, Mitsubishi Power Systems Americas, Mitsubishi Power Systems Europe, MHI Dongfang Gas Turbine (Guangzhou)	②③ MHI Energy & Service, Mitsubishi Nuclear Energy Systems, MHI Plant Construction
	③ Nuclear Energy Systems		
	④ Machinery & Steel Infrastructure Systems	④ MHI Printing & Packaging Machinery, MHI Bridge & Steel Structures Engineering, MHI Mechatronics Systems, MHI Plastic Technology	④ MHI Printing & Packaging Machinery, MHI Bridge & Steel Structures Engineering, MHI Mechatronics Systems, MHI Plastic Technology
	⑤ Aerospace	⑤ Mitsubishi Aircraft, MHI Aerospace Systems, MHI Aerospace Vietnam, MHI	⑤ MHI Logitech, MHI Aero Engine Service
	⑥ General Machinery & Special Vehicles	⑥ Mitsubishi Catepillar Forklift America, Mitsubishi Turbocharger Asia, MHI Equipment Europe	⑥ Mitsubishi Catepillar Forklift America, Mitsubishi Turbocharger Asia, MHI Equipment Europe
	⑦ Air-Conditioning & Refrigeration Systems	⑦ MHI Climate Control, MHI Jinling Air-Conditioners	⑦ MHI Air-Conditioning & Thermal Systems
	⑧ Machine Tools	⑧ MHI Plant Engineering, Ryoin	⑧ MHI Machine Tools Sales, Ryoin

Source: Securities Report for Fiscal Year 2011 and Organization Chart from Homepage.

Table 9: Two corporate groups in the transportation industry and their subsidiaries

	BU Divisions	Subsidiaries
Nihon Yusen	① Liner Trade: Conventional Cargo Transportation Group, Automotive Transportation Headquarters, Car Carrier Group ② Terminal and Harbour Transport: Harbour — Domestic Group, Harbour — Overseas Group ③ Air Cargo Transportation: Air Freight Business Group ④ Logistics: Global Logistics Services Headquarters, Auto-Logistics Group ⑤ Bulk Shipping Services: Dry Bulk Division, Energy Division, Capesize Bulker Group, Handy Bulker Group ⑥ Cruise Ship Services: Cruise Enterprise Group ⑦ Real Estate and Others	① Hinode Line, Astarte Carriers, NYK Line (North America) ② Asahi Unyu, Geneq, Asia Pacific Marine, NYK Terminals, Japan Container Terminal, Yusen Koun ③ Nihon Cargo Airlines ④ Yusen Logistics, Kinkai Yusen Logistics, Camellia Line ⑤ NYK Global Bulk, NYK Bulkship (Asia), NYK Bulkship (Atlantic), Asahi Shipping ⑥ Yusen Cruise, Crystal Cruises ⑦ Yusen Real Estate **Others** NYK Business Systems
Japan Airlines	Air Transportation: Route Marketing Division	Airlines: Japan Airlines, JAL Transocean Air, J-Air, JAL Express, Japan Air Commuter, Ryukyu Air Commuter Sales: JAL Sales, JALPAK, JAL Navia, JAL Mileage Bank Airport Passenger Service: JAL Sky Airport Ground Handling: JAL Ground Service Aircraft Maintenance and Engineering: JAL Engineering Inflight Catering: JAL Royal Catering Cargo and logistics: JAL Cargo Service, Jupiter Global Limited IT: JAL Information Technology

Source: NYK Securities Report for Fiscal Year 2011 and Organization Chart from Homepage.

sections, therefore, I will address the research questions that I have posed initially in Chapter 1 based on the case study findings. Namely, why do corporations establish subsidiaries and form business groups? And how do corporate groups manage their subsidiaries? By answering these questions based on both theory and practice, I hope to contribute to the knowledge of Japanese corporate group management.

6.3 WHY DO FIRMS ESTABLISH SUBSIDIARIES AND FORM CORPORATE GROUPS?

In the literature review provided in Chapter 4, we discussed some of the main theories and literatures concerning why corporations form business groups, and how they draw their firm boundaries. From those theories, we may expect corporate groups to establish and use subsidiaries when:

- External market transaction costs are higher than internal transaction costs within the group.
- Transactions are of high frequency and long periods, complex and have high uncertainty, hard to evaluate and measure, related to other assets and production such that changes require difficult coordination beyond firm boundary.
- Subsidiaries effectively balance external market transaction costs and otherwise high internal transaction costs that incur from a decrease in production as a result of excessive control.
- It matters to have residual control rights over what cannot be specified *ex ante* in contracts which are by nature incomplete, especially when it concerns relationship specific investments that are important to the company.
- There is complementarity of related assets. In other words when relation specific assets of the parent do not create value unless employed with the related assets owned by the subsidiary company.
- Capabilities need to be acquired internally rather than through the market. For example, when tacit knowledge is needed within the corporate group to help reduce costs of integrating across diverse production capabilities and activities.

- It is possible and necessary to use decentralization as a means to solve incentive problems related to *ex-ante* commitment by management not to interfere (and thereby curb incentives of business divisions) *ex-post*.
- Power delegation is necessary to cope with increasingly diversified and complex businesses, to have clear accountability, to speed up decision making, and to foster development of new logic and competencies that are needed to fuel growth in new businesses.
- It is necessary from an HR perspective to have flexible usage of labour cost structure, and to provide senior positions to employees of the parent company.

Many findings from the case study appear to be partially or generally consistent with the above mentioned theories. For example, both Hitachi and Panasonic use the company system to delegate decision rights to their in-house companies and subsidiaries so as to allow swifter decision making and to enhance entrepreneurism as well as accountability. A manager at Panasonic describes the delegation to business divisions and subsidiaries as follows:

"The creation and use of business division has been very much a key management principle of Panasonic's founder Konosuke Mastashita, who believed that employees learn and acquire competencies through business activities. For example, a manager responsible for his business division has to identify market opportunities, invest in R&D, develop and market products, manage product life cycle as well as customer relations. Other employees too are involved in managing and creating value, and it is through these activities of creating new products and entering into new markets by business divisions and subsidiaries that Panasonic grew to be what it is today."

The case studies, however, revealed some other noteworthy aspects concerning the use of subsidiaries. In this and the following sections, I will try to highlight some of the aspects.

(a) *Ex-post* Lock-in of Group Boundary

Firstly, although firms are careful about transactions costs in their make or buy decisions, once they have decided on establishing a subsidiary, and investments have been made, they are likely to face a certain lock-in situation where it becomes hard to switch from using the subsidiary to using the market, even when external transactions costs are lower than internal transaction costs. In other words, at least in the short term, after a subsidiary has been established, transaction cost is not the sole defining factor that determines make or buy decisions *ex-post*. A manager at Hitachi's head-office described the situation as follows:

> "Once we have built a subsidiary, say for example a manufacturing plant, it is not just costs that we have to consider, but also utilization rate of the subsidiary. It is not conceivable that we will outsource to external manufacturers when our own manufacturing subsidiary is underutilized and has the capacity to produce the required amount. This is not favoritism, but a matter of maintaining a certain acceptable level of utilization of the corporate group's resources and tangible assets. Therefore, both factors of cost and utilization, as well as the resulting business performance have to be considered. Careful consideration is especially necessary when switching costs are high."

The perception of lock-in may be affected by mental accounting and bounded rationality, which make the decision maker justify the lock-in of high input costs of subsidiaries. All five corporate groups said they generally apply a market price principle towards transactions with their subsidiaries. In other words, prices paid to subsidiaries for inputs are essentially based on market prices for the equivalent good or service. But in reality, it seems improbable that there exists market price for all inputs, especially when they are highly firm specific such that there are virtually no alternatives in the market to allow comparison. For highly firm specific inputs, not only is it difficult to determine a fair market price, but it is also easy to justify paying a premium for the supposedly customized and hence superior inputs of high quality. This is especially true if the inputs provided by a subsidiary that constitutes an important part of the firm's core competencies.

Although possibly not prevalent among the case study groups, some firms I have talked to appear to adopt a rather indifferent attitude towards the price they paid to their subsidiaries. One reason that is often cited is that under consolidated financial accounting, parent–subsidiary transactions are cross-cancelled, such that high input costs are sometimes permissible because there is no actual cash outflow from the corporate group. A manager I talked to described its firm's relation with its former parent company as follows:

> "Previously, when we were Company X's subsidiary, our parent company has not been strict on the price we charged them for our products and services. But after we have been acquired by another corporate group and thence ceased to be Company X's subsidiary, Company X revised its trading terms with us. Today, our transactions are strictly based on market price."

Three insights can be derived from this issue of lock-in. Firstly, the existence of lock-in may depend on type of subsidiary and its relationship with the parent. There has to be some dependency relationship, otherwise the parent can just divest the subsidiary and remove all undesirable lock-in risks. A lock-in would be harder to unknot if the parent and subsidiary are mutual dependent on each other's output.

Secondly, lock-in may produce or prolong inefficiencies when governance mechanisms fail to detect inefficiencies and re-evaluate the role of subsidiaries. For example, in a parent–subsidiary relationship where the parent has for years depended on its subsidiary for production inputs, what has become routine transaction may breed problems that affect performance. Cost planning may be based on the previous year's cost figures marked up or down, rather than based on competitive market price comparisons. In order to evaluate appropriately whether a subsidiary is efficient or not, it is necessary first to have a clear understanding as to the role of the subsidiary, and how it is expected to contribute to the corporate group. Many firms that I have talked to appear to having problems defining or re-defining the mission of their subsidiaries and evaluating their performances. And as a result it is not always clear to them as to whether the existing boundary should be maintained, or whether it should be redrawn.

Thirdly, because of lock-in situations that arise after a subsidiary has been established, group boundary may not be as flexible as assumed by the transaction cost theory. If, according to theory, the economic rationale of Japanese companies' use of a parent–subsidiary form of governance is to balance transaction costs, then caution will be needed if there exists a possibility of *ex-post* lock-in, and scenarios where internal transaction costs substantially outweigh external transaction costs need to be considered and taken into account.

(b) Balancing Centripetal and Centrifugal Forces

Incentive theory suggests that subsidiaries are used as a means of signalling commitment by the parent not to interfere *ex-post*, such that the business divisions will have the *ex-ante* incentives to invest in firm specific efforts without having to worry that management will renege on their promises and interfere with their decisions. This idea applies also to the use of subsidiaries to balance high external transaction costs and high internal transaction costs that are caused by excessive management interference and control which decreases productivity.

Although corporations establish subsidiaries and make use of their centrifugal incentives to expand businesses as theory suggests, the case studies also show that companies apply centripetal forces to balance centrifugal forces and to ensure that the group's overall strategic goals are met. This in evident in the multiple coordination systems that are typically used in large corporate groups for controlling subsidiaries. In balancing centrifugal and centripetal forces, emphasis is often placed on mutual agreement between parent and subsidiary so as not to damage incentives.

Coordinating centripetally would sometimes entail taking over a business unit that belongs to a subsidiary, as was the case with Hitachi, which announced in December 2012 that it would take over the car information system business from its subsidiary Hitachi Automotive Device Systems. Hitachi's main reason for doing so was because the system was seen as a crucial key in realizing the company's plan to fortify their next generation Smart City capabilities within its social infrastructure business.

Sometimes, in order to strengthen synergies within a corporate group, even subsidiaries that have become publicly listed companies would be delisted so that the parent company, in acquiring full ownership, could restructure or strengthen the group's businesses.

For example, in 2011, we witnessed Panasonic's full ownership of Panasonic Electric Works, and in 2012, Hitachi Solutions' full ownership of Hitachi Business Solution, and Hitachi Metals' full ownership of Hitachi Tool. Although incentive issues are being considered, and pioneer spirit encouraged, the extent to which the corporate group tilts centripetally or centrifugally depends also on the way in which the group coordinates its activities in response to changes in its business environment. However, if centripetal coordination decreases productivity, as the theory of balancing transaction cost posits, then such coordination would entail trade-offs between coordination benefits and productivity losses.

It is arguable that such trade-offs might not always be great, and changing to a 100% ownership does not necessarily mean that centripetal coordination by the parent would always damage incentives and reduce productivity. But even if they are substantial, the business environment a corporate group faces may deem it necessary to make such a strategic move. In which case, it follows that the economic rationale of using or not subsidiaries is not restricted to balancing internal and external transaction costs, but includes also the benefits of allowing the parent company to cherry pick from a broader set of strategic options, namely amongst using in-house organizations, subsidiaries, and the market, as well as the corresponding control and coordination system that follows the chosen option, as shown in Figure 14.

(c) Knowledge defines the Group Boundary

In Chapter 4, we discussed that tacit knowledge makes trading of capabilities difficult, and this, in turn, may determine the group boundary. Especially when businesses are diverse, cognitive constraints deems it necessary for divisions to specialize in their respective areas, and subsidiaries are often used to fulfil this role. But the cost of integrating across diverse capabilities may outweigh transaction costs, and firms will then determine what is to be done inside the group, and what is to be outsourced.

However, the cases revealed that the amount of tacit knowledge that is required depends on the work that is involved. Less tacit knowledge is required in a standardized and modularized production

Parent Company	**Subsidiary Company**	**Market Transaction**
Choose in-house division or subsidiary when external transaction cost is high. The parent also chooses an appropriate level of control. But if the cost of integration outweighs transaction costs, the parent will choose to use the market.	In addition to balancing internal and external transaction costs, the parent may choose to exercise its hierarchical control rights, or use its subsidiary as one of many suppliers in the market.	Choose market when transaction costs are lower, and when there is little risk of *ex-post* opportunistic behaviour or uncertainties. In many cases the cost of using the market can be prohibitively high.

Figure 14: Choice between in-house, subsidiary, and market revisited

setting, while a certain amount of tacit knowledge is required to combine vast numbers of highly specialized tasks. A greater level of tacit knowledge is also required for craftsmanship related work and *suriawase* (close coordination) style production that many Japanese manufacturers are known for.

Although there may be variance amongst industries, from the case studies at least, it appears that tacit and explicit knowledge are shared through working together regardless of whether the party concerned is a subsidiary or an external partner such as a *keiretsu* supplier. As a manager from Hitachi describes, "Knowledge is vital. All designs and materials that are used in manufacturing have to be approved in advance. No company can show up suddenly and become our supplier. It has to meet our required qualifications first." So although knowledge draws the firm boundary as theory suggests, the "firm" here is a wider business group that includes relational business partners.

One implication that can be derived from this idea of knowledge as boundary is that investments made in building and sharing knowledge with subsidiaries as well as external partners and suppliers, could raise switching costs and create a locked-in situation where production efficiency and performances could in due course turn out to be sub-optimal, especially when there are other production technologies outside the group that are working towards establishing different industry standards. In other words, a corporate group could become organizationally too rigid as a result of lock-in if knowledge is not benchmarked against external best practices.

(d) Strategic Necessity for Having Subsidiaries

Contingency theory posits that there is no best way to organize a corporation, and that the optimal course of action is contingent upon the company's internal and external environment. In other words, structure follows strategy, which is tailored and adjusted in response to the environment the company faces. The case studies identified many examples of strategic necessities for having subsidiaries.

(a) Vertical integration when production inputs that cannot be procured from the market.

A company may need certain inputs for production, but because of reasons such as small batch size, the company may not be able to find a supplier to supply it with the required inputs. Such was the case in the early years of Hitachi, when the company was still relatively small, and it was not always easy then to have suppliers sell Hitachi small batches of production inputs and materials. Hitachi, therefore, had to produce those inputs internally. Many of those manufacturing units subsequently grew and become Hitachi's subsidiaries. Integrating vertically was more a matter of necessity than of choice when producing internally was the only means to stably secure the firm's required production inputs.

(b) Use subsidiaries to meet legal requirements.

Subsidiaries may be established to meet legal requirements or to allow business operations in different countries. In the case of Nihon Yusen, which has hundreds of foreign subsidiaries established as special purpose companies in order to register liner vessels under different nationalities, the subsidiaries were created so that Nihon Yusen could execute its strategy for its liner business.

We see this also in the aviation industry which is still heavily regulated. Unless there is an open sky agreement or approved bilateral traffic and capacity rights, the only way to set up an airline operation to fly from a third country to another is to establish an airline in the originating third country.

(c) Use subsidiaries to shape or alter the competitive environment.

Subsidiaries may also be used, as commented by Hitachi's manager, as an entrenchment strategy to create competitive advantage by, for example, monopolizing or having control over production capabilities and resources of important production inputs or products. Sometimes subsidiaries are also used to enhance the perception of being a neutral and unbiased supplier or service provider that services both the parent company and its rivals.

(d) Use subsidiaries to develop identified business opportunities.

Subsidiaries are often established as new ventures to capture and develop new business opportunities that have been identified. Hitachi describes their situation as follows:

> "It is hard to generalize all situations, but typically it would result from an identification of opportunities, competencies and synergies. For example, we might want to establish a subsidiary that manufactures semi-conductors in a rural district. Land and labour are relatively cheap. The region also has many skilled talents that we can hire, but capital and production knowledge are required. Capital can be raised at lower costs through Hitachi, and production know-how can be transferred from Hitachi to the new subsidiary."

A specific region or country may provide new entrant firms certain advantages, such as the ease of recruiting skilled employees and of utilizing established R&D functions. These advantages offer firms the incentives to establish subsidiaries in the region. The use of subsidiaries in developing new ventures may be effective in containing risks should the venture fail, or as K. Ito (1996) describes, in producing offspring that would improve the chance of the company's continual survival.

(e) Respond to host country demands.

Although there has to be some underlying business prospects, the strategic necessity of forming subsidiaries may also arise from local demands of the host country in which the company operates its business. A general manager of Panasonic describes the situation as follows:

> "Initially we manufactured products in Japan and had our overseas marketing and sales subsidiary launch the products in that region. But later we were faced with pressures from the host country where we were asked to build factories. Manufacturing subsidiaries were subsequently established and their numbers increased. In some cases, because manufacturing assembly alone does not transfer knowledge and technology, we were further asked to develop R&D capabilities in the host country. The extent to which we establish subsidiaries often depends on business conditions and requirements."

(f) Tailor offering to meet customer demand.

Even in the event when a corporation can procure all of its production inputs from the market instead of producing them in-house by a subsidiary, it may still choose to own the production function so that it could understand customer needs better and be able to tailor offerings that would be more relevant to its customers. Such was the case with Nihon Yusen, which uses external forwarders extensively for their container liner business, but yet maintains its own logistics subsidiaries so that it could understand better and meet customers' needs by tailoring logistics offerings.

There are other strategic necessities in addition to those mentioned above. Appendix-2 gives a summary of 126 news releases concerning reasons for establishing subsidiaries, over the period from 1st January to 31st December 2012. The articles in the data set mention the identification of growing markets and business opportunities, the development of businesses or capabilities, and the function the established subsidiary will perform. Of strategic necessity, the articles mention the use of subsidiaries, as a means to enter or expand penetration into markets that have growth potential, to gain access or have ownership over scarce resources, such as natural gas mining rights, and to develop synergies or acquire competencies.

Whatever the strategic reasons are, once a company expands it boundary by creating subsidiaries, then there is a potential risk that a parent–subsidiary lock-in may occur. And because of this, the management of subsidiaries, including the *ex-post* evaluation or re-evaluation of their performance and roles, should be treated as an integral part of a business group's strategy execution. Just how well do companies actually manage their subsidiaries? This is a theme which I will discuss in the next section. But given the economic rationale and the many reasons that firms have for using subsidiaries, to what extent is this mode of governance distinctly Japanese? K. Ito (1996), noted in his comparison between Japan and the US that firstly, the cost of managing subsidiaries is higher in the US where contracting cost is high, while such cost is lower in Japan. Secondly, while giving more autonomy may induce shirking in the US, there is less such worry in Japan because of a social network that limits and punishes opportunism.

In addition to the above two aspects, one could add a third, and that is the community firm aspect of Japanese corporations. Many senior management personnel in subsidiary companies are staff who are seconded or transferred from the parent company, thus providing senior positions to capable staff when such positions are limited in the parent company; and in doing so maintain a motivated workforce as well as train future leaders by providing them an opportunity to experience senior roles in subsidiaries. There is also a paternal element of ensuring that the subsidiary will have human resource capable of managing the subsidiary's business as well as align incentives with that of the parent company. However, the credibility of this strategy is arguable, although many Japanese firms find it effective.

A research by Miyamoto (2006), for example, showed that the percentage of firms using secondments has increased, and in year 2000, 97.8% of companies that have over 5,000 employees have used secondments. Miyamoto's case study was on a corporate group in the manufacturing sector, in which the parent company and its 52 out of 106 domestic subsidiaries were studied. The study showed that secondment had a positive relation with an increase in labour productivity and profitability. These benefits were brought about by the production knowledge and skills that were transferred from the parent company to the subsidiary through secondments. The mutual benefits that can be gained make this form of governance viable and widely adopted.

6.4 HOW DO CORPORATE GROUPS MANAGE THEIR SUBSIDIARIES?

In Chapter 5, we discussed theories and issues concerning the management of subsidiaries, such as the delegation of decision rights and trade-offs between costs and benefits of decentralization. We also looked at hybrid coordination in companies where skilled workers adjust management's instructions using local information. We discussed dual pressures and conflict between parent companies and subsidiaries and how some level of self-enforcing governance can be achieved through repeated interactions. In this section, we will look further into understanding how corporate groups manage their subsidiaries by drawing from findings obtained from the case studies, and compare them to major academic theories.

6.4.1 Vertical and Horizontal Coordination Systems

I begin by describing the coordination systems that are found in the case study companies and see how they function in planning, executing strategy, and maintaining the group's overall optimality.

Coordination systems within large corporate groups

Owan and Kato's theory on vertical and horizontal coordination system described in Chapter 5 highlights very adequately the importance of and the difficulty in executing strategy whilst making at the same time necessary adjustments based on local information in order to make better and prompter decisions that are responsive to changes in business environments. This is especially relevant in large corporate groups that have numerous layers of business divisions and subsidiaries. Although there are numerous differences amongst the five corporate groups concerning how they organize the management of their numerous subsidiaries, what is common is that they have control and coordination systems that enable the parent company to coordinate vertically as well as horizontally with its subsidiaries. Their major characteristics are as follows:

(a) Counterpart Head-Office Department

Each subsidiary has one or several counterpart departments in the parent company. This may be a department within an in-house company (Hitachi and Panasonic), a business division, or a department that works alongside the subsidiary, depending on the nature and role of the subsidiary. The parent department coordinates with its subsidiaries to communicate strategic goals, to discuss operational issues and to monitor activities.

(b) Group Management Department

One or multiple group management departments oversee and support subsidiaries horizontally across the business group. Their roles range from monitoring performance to providing management and compliance rules and guidelines.

(c) Functional Meetings

Functional meetings for head of, for example, accounting, general affairs, HR, R&D would gather to discuss issues, exchange ideas, and share information. It also gives the parent head-office the opportunity to disseminate information to all subsidiaries concerned. There are also performance report meetings to monitor performance gaps and to discuss ways to dress them.

(d) Personnel Rotation, Secondments and Transfers

It is not rare that the senior management positions in the subsidiaries are partly filled by personnel seconded or transferred from the parent company. Although there is an element of absorbing excessively labour from the parent company, such secondment and transfer enable not only control and influence by the parent company, but also a means through which pressures from both the parent and the subsidiary can be mediated. This is because the seconded or transferred person understands both the strategic direction of the head-office as well as local information that is not always visible to the head-office, and is thus capable of acting as a mediator. There are also personnel rotations across divisions and subsidiaries that allow managers to acquire knowledge concerning how other related functions work, and to create networks that facilitate cross-function efforts such as coordination amongst production, product design and sales.

Figure 15 depicts the typical vertical and horizontal coordination system found in many Japanese corporate groups.

To illustrate how the coordination systems described above works, I will use one of the case study corporate groups as an example. Figure 16 shows how the MHI Group organizes the control and coordination of its subsidiaries.

Within Business Division A is a manufacturing subsidiary X that builds ships. There are multiple managing departments that together coordinate activities performed by Subsidiary X. While it is the Engineering Department that oversees Subsidiary X's daily operation, it is the subsidiary's management department aided by the Planning Department that oversees its business performance, while the head of Business Division A is responsible for the overall business performance of the entire division. The department that acts as Subsidiary X's management department depends on the role of the subsidiary. The Corporate Planning Department makes sure that the

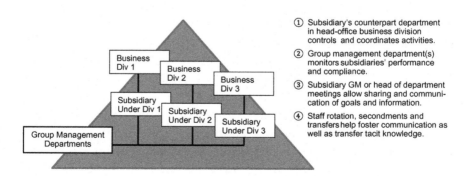

Figure 15:   Organizational control and coordination systems of a corporate group

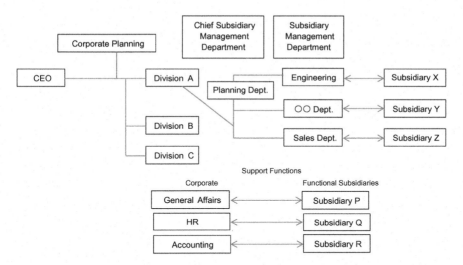

Figure 16: Control and coordination of subsidiaries at MHI

organizational design is optimal and that that the departments and subsidiaries function as intended. In addition to the above, there are also corporate support departments such as HR, Accounting, and General Affairs that provide the division with specialized functions.

Similarly, Hitachi, Panasonic, Nihon Yusen and Japan Airlines too have head-office departments that monitor and coordinate activities of their subsidiaries. For each subsidiary, there is usually a counterpart department within the head office that is responsible for this role. This counterpart or managing department performs, borrowing the term from Owan and Kato (2008), hybrid coordination because it aggregates local information of the subsidiaries that it oversees, and coordinates activities to ensure that they are aligned with vertical controls and strategy execution.

In addition to the subsidiary counterpart or managing department of the business division, there are also head-office departments that exert governance across business divisions and their subsidiaries. In Nihon Yusen for example, the Group Management Committee decides on the basic management policies and compliance rules that are to be applied across all subsidiaries.

The corporate group's mid-term and annual targets, strategic goals and company policies are often conveyed to subsidiaries through joint conferences. In Panasonic, where each business unit has its own head of HR, head of accounting and head of planning, there are heads of accounting meetings, head of planning meetings and so forth, where all the heads of department from the head-office and wholly owned subsidiaries gather to share information and discuss policies. For example, there are around 50–60 heads of accounting in Panasonic, and they often rotate amongst accounting departments such that the head of accounting in company A becomes head of accounting in subsidiary B, head of accounting in subsidiary B moves to the role of heads of accounting in subsidiary C, and so forth. In Japan Airlines too, all the heads of general affairs departments are summoned to attend meetings, where information concerning policies and governance are shared and discussed.

As described in the previous section, secondments and transfers of managers from the parent company to the subsidiary, as well as secondments of staffs from the subsidiary to the parent company are widely used practices. Cross-secondments help foster communication, transfer knowledge, and allow the parent company to exert influence, where necessary over the subsidiary's actions. They provide opportunities for the parent company to train its managers, and have them exposed to top management roles in subsidiaries before they assume senior positions in the head office, while it also allows the subsidiary to learn and share the values of the parent company.

Despite their many benefits, one may still wonder whether such coordination systems slow down or speed up decision making. The answer to this question depends on the amount of coordination that is required, and that in turn often depends on the type of subsidiary. Because subsidiaries are created to speed up decision making and save communication costs, as we have discussed earlier in this book, autonomous business subsidiaries may require less coordination, and coordination may be used only on areas that affect the corporate group's overall performance. On the other hand, for subsidiaries that are integrated into the parent company's production value chain, routine will often involve more close coordination between parent and subsidiary.

Although coordination requires time and effort, it aligns expectations such that work can be carried out smoothly with little corrections.

Coordination in planning, execution and adjustment, optimization

Having discussed the main coordination systems, we now look at how they are used in the coordination of activities. Given that most large corporate groups have some form of system in place for controlling and coordinating activities vertically and horizontally, the question remains as to whether these systems are effective. Is local information concerning customer trends and competitive environment promptly collected and analyzed? Are activities across the organization adjusted quickly and coherently to capture business chance or mitigate risks? In large corporate groups, deciding everything centrally is inefficient and impermissible cost-wise. So despite some degrees of control losses, appropriate levels of delegation complemented with monitoring are used to minimize control losses. In the case study, I observed how corporate head-offices play an important role in the coordination of (a) planning, (b) strategy execution and adjustments, and (c) optimization of activities within the corporate group.

(a) Coordination in Planning

Regarding planning, the coordination system observed in the case study entails aggregating local information in a bottom-up manner, after which cost and output decisions flows down the organizational hierarchy. This resembles the technology posited by Mookherjee for using decentralization to obtain the same expected outcomes as an optimal centralized setting (as described in Section 5.1). A manager at MHI describes their coordination as follows:

> "It is both top-down as well as bottom-up. The corporate head-office drafts the strategic big picture concerning how they want the corporation to move forward. Each business division, together with their subsidiaries, then work out how the strategic goals related to its division could be achieved by drafting business plans. The plans are

then aggregated by the head-office, and if the planned forecasts do not meet the strategic goals including SVA (EVA) targets, the business divisions will be asked to work out again ways to fill the gap."

Likewise, this combination of top–down and bottom–up approach is also used in Hitachi's planning process. A manager at Hitachi describes their coordination as follows:

"In our budgeting process, the top sets out the vision and strategic direction, and the budgeting of, for example, sales plan and costs are all worked out bottom-up. The important coordination here is to have the bottom agree on the budget before the figures are aggregated bottom-up. The resulting budget is, therefore, not a target but a promise. And because it is a promise, everyone expects it to be kept. In other words, the corporate strategy is based on sound bottom commitment. The strength of this bottom-up culture is evident in the post 3.11 earthquake, when it contributed greatly to prompt and coordinated actions."

This process of aggregating information to form a strategic plan is an important coordination activity because it allows the organization to make more informed decisions based on realistic plans, even though plans are based on assumptions that may change as the business environment changes. But because the plans are at least checked in terms of realistic feasibility, they highlight gaps where the proposed plans fail to meet the corporate strategic goals, and thereby allow the organization to make adjustments or build new competencies in order to fill the gaps that have been identified. It also allows the organization to check if the plans are strategically consistent with other plans and goals that make up the corporate strategy, or whether there are duplicated activities that could be combined and thereby increase efficiency or save costs.

However, if done without reflecting reality, this coordination process could lead to serious problems. For example, if plans that have been submitted are strict commitments, a subsidiary may either push itself beyond its capability in supplying cheaply to the parent company and ends up suffering losses. Or, being too risk averse, it may submit easily attainable targets to avoid noticeable failures. The quality of the plan, therefore, depends on the subsidiary's attitude towards its commitment, and also the coordinator's ability in each aggregation stage to judge whether the reported bottom–up plan is indeed appropriate and acceptable. This will not be easy if the coordinator lacks knowledge about the subsidiary and cannot judge appropriately the quality of the reported plans.

Ineffective coordination could also lead to what I would describe as "wishful thinking plans" and "stapled plans". Wishful thinking plans are plans that lack substance and realistic forecast but yet everyone wishes earnestly that events will somehow miraculously unfold as planned. Often because of dysfunctional coordination, such organizations will have difficulty identifying the root of their problems when events begin to do diverge from what was planned, and as a result, corrective actions will also be late or ineffective. Stapled plans are bottom–up plans of "what each department says they want to do" stapled together. Such plans often lack consistency and have conflicting goals. For example, the product development department may define the core product as premium, while the manufacturing department may produce them as non-frill to save costs, and the sales department may reduce price to reach its sales volume quota, such that the front-line staffs will be left confused as to what the company's strategy really is.

It is, therefore, important to have effective coordination systems such as cross-functional coordinators who understand decision trade-offs, and who is capable of ensuring that the strategic plan is coordinated in such a way that it can be effectively executed across the organization. It may, however, be hard for large corporations to have sufficient staffs trained as effective coordinators. I recently came across a corporate survey that was conducted on 500 head-office managers. It revealed that one of the required skills managers felt they lack most was coordination skill, and in particular, knowledge of other department's work and how they are related to create value. It is also important to assign an appropriate department as the subsidiary's head-office counter-part. In one of the case study companies, a certain head-office department was assigned because the subsidiary was initially a part of that department's value chain. But years later, even after the subsidiary's role has shifted such that a different department would have been more suitable as the counter-part, the assignment has not been revised. As a result, control and coordination became ceremonial rather than effective as originally intended.

(b) Execution and Adjustment

All the companies in the case study have a relatively high degree of decentralization, which is complemented with PDCA (Plan-Do-Check-Action) systems that monitor the effectiveness of activities within the corporate group. Because of consolidated financial reporting and quarterly disclosure of financial results, companies monitor performance progress against profit forecasts announced for the fiscal year. Performance control is a crucial activity essential for identifying lagging areas and for taking corrective measures promptly. As a head-office manager in one of the case study companies describes, "Problems will reveal themselves in the financial results and they will be questioned. They will also be rectified subsequently through the business division's PDCA cycle."

In the case of Hitachi, although an individual business subsidiary is responsible for its own business plans, if the performance deviates from what was planned, resulting in excessive production and left over inventory that would affect consolidated performance, the corporate department will step in to interfere and exert control. The corporate department would inquire the causes of discrepancy, and question the premises under which the subsidiary initially made its investment and production decisions, as well as premises under which the corrective measures are said to work. As a manager in Hitachi describes,

> "There are two levels of governance, one at the subsidiary level, and one at the group corporate head-office. It is fine if the investment generates profits, but does it really? ... is the kind of question we ask. We also check the premise and evidence that justifies the investment decision. In our monthly monitoring, we question things such as: Why has inventory level risen? Why has asset utilization dropped? Such that

gaps are identified and usually rectified within two to three months. Serious problems however are escalated and discussed at a higher level. Each level is responsible to its shareholder, the subsidiary to its parent, the parent to its in-house company, and Hitachi to its shareholders. This governance system works in this way throughout all layers within the organization."

This system of monthly or quarterly monitoring of performance gaps, and of identifying causes and rectifying discrepancies, appears to be a very widely adopted practice in many companies. Unfortunately, I was not able to extract much information from the case study companies regarding performance outcome, and for the information I have succeeded in obtaining, I am not allowed to disclose them. However, there are other companies that I have talked to outside the case study companies, who admitted to having problems evaluating their subsidiaries. For example, one corporate head-office manager said to me,

"One difficulty is managing performance based on the mission of the subsidiary that is being evaluated. Very often the mission is not the same as when the subsidiary was initially established. It is also not realistic to apply the same financial KPIs such as ROA across all subsidiaries when they are essentially very different in the functions they perform. Another difficulty comes with deciding under what circumstances and to what extent should the corporate head-office step in and interfere, and when not to."

A problem I noticed in the case studies is that although companies have some form of classification, there does not appear to be much difference in ways subsidiaries are controlled and managed despite their varying characteristics. I posit, therefore, that subsidiaries should be categorized and managed according to their roles and relationship with their parent company. Subsidiary type should therefore be considered when deciding which performance measure to use. If it is a business subsidiary that is expected to contribute to consolidated earnings, then it may be appropriate to set KPIs based on for example the number of new clients or profit per customer segment. If, however, it is a purely functional subsidiary that works more as a cost centre, then things like operation costs saved, productivity, and service quality level may be more appropriate as performance measures.

(c) Achieving Overall Optimality

The third area of coordination concerns overall optimization to ensure that partial optimization within each division or business units sums up to be optimal as a whole. Many literatures, such as Fujii and Matsuzaki's book "Management and Learning in Japanese Corporations (2004)", mention the issues of conglomerate discount and fallacy of composition. There have also been empirical studies, such as NLI Research Institute's analysis (2003) of 9,159 company data, which show that performance turns negative when hiving-off of subsidiaries exceeds a certain threshold. So at some point, someone has to step back a little and look at the big picture to see if the present way is truly the right way of organizing activities and executing strategy.

This overall optimality is precisely one of the key stresses of Japan's famous Amoeba Management System, which was developed by the Japanese business guru Dr. Kazuo Inamori, and which was introduced to Japan Airlines as part of its restructure plan. Although activities are divided and delegated to the smallest possible units, with each unit being held responsible for its own profit and loss, the system also ensures that partial optimality is translated to overall optimality. In what is called a Micro-Macro Loop, all activities are clustered into loops so as to make explicitly clear as to which activity affects which, and how together they can produce intended and desired results.

As an outcome of coordination for overall optimization, business units and divisions may be re-grouped differently to enhance cross-divisional synergies, or the corporate pendulum may swing in preference towards a more centralized rather than decentralized decision making structure.

It is not always easy to judge whether what is deemed optimal by the head-office management indeed leads to better results. There are sceptics who argue that fiddling with structure misses the point that the problem lies not in structure but in Japanese manufacturers' inability to come up with appealing and relevant products in a globalized market. Recent corporate restructurings in Japan, however, suggest that in a globalized, commoditized and modularized world of manufacturing at least, a "laissez-faire and let them flourish" approach to subsidiary management does not fit the current business environment, and that a more centralized approach is needed to redefine the corporate mission and re-group competencies to create focus and synergy.

In MHI for example, businesses are grouped into four domains to enhance synergies amongst business units. A manager at MHI describes,

> "We produce automotive products such as turbo charge, engine bulb and car air-conditioning, and it makes sense to group all these activities together under the key-word automobile. In the past, a business division would go to a client not realizing that another related business division from MHI has recently been there. Today, related activities are grouped in a way such that we can now propose and deliver packaged solutions to our clients."

Hitachi too has steered away from its past image of electronics and home appliance manufacturer, and has instead been focusing successfully on its social infrastructure businesses such as power plant and transport systems that links or integrates core competencies and synergies of its business divisions and subsidiaries.

Panasonic too, facing commoditization and crumbling prices in its core business of digital home appliances, has decided to reinvent the company and shift away from manufacturing and selling products to becoming a solution provider, which would allow Panasonic to bring together and link the many products and services the group has to propose and deliver value added solutions.

Panasonic has a few years ago announced to restructure itself. From April 1st 2013, the company decided to revive its business division structure, which was abolished 12 years ago. The business division structure was introduced to Panasonic in 1933 by its founder Konosuke Matsushita. Each product was managed from product development to production and sales as a division, and these businesses divisions grew rapidly and successfully as they competed against themselves. But in just half a century, as more and more new products emerged, the number of business divisions grew to over a hundred, with different divisions marketing their own brands of essentially a same product. There were, for example, three divisions developing their own digital cameras, and it was apparent that such duplications are not efficient utilization of scare corporate resources. It was, therefore, deemed rational, for example, to combine the divisions of radio, stereo and tape recorder into one audio division. While for areas that require substantial investment in R&D such as video and semi-conductor, it was considered better for the corporate head-office to manage them as projects. In 2001, the then CEO Kunio Nakamura abolished the business division structure, and restructured the organization according to its functions such as planning and development, manufacturing, marketing and sales. He also re-grouped the former divisions and subsidiaries into 14 business domains. The 14 domains were subsequently re-grouped into nine domains.

But since then, times and circumstances have again changed. Prior to April 1st 2013, Panasonic had 88 Business Units responsible for planning and development, but most of them had separate manufacturing and sales departments, such that information from manufacturing and sales were not easily incorporated into product development processes. Under the leadership of the present CEO Kazuhiro Tsuga, the Business Units were reduced from 88 to 49 in April 2013, and they were renamed as Business Divisions and given the responsibility to centrally control all functions. The New Medium Term Business Plan, which was announced on 28th March 2013, defined the responsibility of global development, production and sales as follows: "Henceforth, the person who produces will need to think how to market, and to see through the sales of their products." In addition, each business division is also expected to be responsible for managing its own balance sheet, in other words for continuously increasing cash and profit. For large scale business development projects that require resources a business division alone cannot secure, the four in-house companies (Appliance, AVC Networks, Eco Solutions and Automotive and Industrial Systems) will support such business developments. Key words in the new plan include "Cross Value Innovation", which emphasizes the direction towards creating synergies by customizing Panasonic's core competencies to wherever possible in its business portfolio, and "Engineering a Better World for You" which aims to reinvent Panasonic's value proposition as an industrial partner and a provider of quality life.

These examples of MHI, Hitachi and Panasonic illustrate that attaining over optimality through managing changes and regrouping subsidiaries is very much a top management priority, where the head-office plays an important role in coordinating strategy execution.

6.4.2 Delegation of Decision Rights to Subsidiaries

Vertical and horizontal coordination systems are closely related to how decision rights are being delegated to business divisions and subsidiaries within a corporate group. Although large corporate groups with diverse businesses across multiple regions require some level of delegation to enable prompt decision making, it does not necessarily mean that once decision rights have been delegated, coordination is no longer required. On the contrary, as Miyajima and Aoki have argued, delegation needs to be complemented with sufficient monitoring so as to minimize agency problems and control loss. A subsidiary company may be delegated decision rights over daily routine operation, but may still coordinate actively with its counterpart head-office department to work on better ways of improving product quality or giving feedbacks concerning customer satisfaction. In other words, delegation and coordination may often be used together to manage subsidiaries.

But such a combination of delegation and coordination elicits the question as to whether coordination will be seen by the subsidiary as undesirable interference, and hence lead to the kind of decrease in productivity that incentive theorists posit? If, as posited by Ito *et al.* (1997), subsidiaries are used as a means to solve incentive problems (because once decision rights have been delegated to its subsidiary, the parent company cannot easily renege on its promise of not to interfere), why then do we observe frequent occasions where the head-office interferes with decisions made by the subsidiaries?

From an incentive perspective, does interference not defeat the purpose of establishing subsidiaries? How do we reconcile theory with
practice?

Indeed, we find a high degree of autonomy in the case study
companies such as Hitachi and Panasonic, whose subsidiaries are
often encouraged to be pioneers in their specialized fields whilst being
also responsible for their profits and losses. But at the same time,
because the performance a subsidiary can have substantial impact on
the consolidated performance of the whole corporate group, and
because internal control is mandatory by company law, we also see
parent companies exercising control over their subsidiaries. There
appears, therefore, to be dual pressures, where the parent company
needs to delegate in order to enhance incentives, but also to have
control in order to maintain appropriate governance.

All five corporations in the case study have rules and guidelines
that define the delegation of decision rights to subsidiaries, such that
it is relatively clear as to when and to what extent a subsidiary can
make decisions at its own discretion, and when it requires prior
approval from the corporate head-office. It is because of these rules
on the delegation of decision rights that subsidiaries are capable of
knowing *ex-ante* the amount of discretion they have, and hence avoid
situations where their decisions would be over-ridden *ex-post* by the
parent company. Although it is arguable that despite the clear rules,
subsidiaries may still be dissatisfied with the limited level of power
delegation and may feel that the controls are excessive or that the parent company is underestimating their capabilities, hence resulting in
incentive problems again, knowing how to play by the rules at least
enables the subsidiaries to form accurate expectations *ex-ante*.

From the case studies, I observed that parent companies tend
to exert more control over their subsidiaries under the following
circumstances:

• When the subsidiary begins to show poor performance. In
  Hitachi, delegation of decision rights depends on the corporate
  ranking of the subsidiary's performance. What Hitachi calls an
  FIV (Future Inspiration Value) is used to evaluate subsidiaries

based on operating profit and cash flow. A manager at Hitachi describes the ranking of subsidiaries as follows:

> "It depends on performance. Generally speaking when things are fine we leave things to our subsidiaries and have them report to us where necessary afterwards. But when performance is poor, delegated decision rights become smaller, and such subsidiaries will be asked to report their results monthly so that we can monitor more closely and frequently. Using the analogy of a medical check-up, the patient will be sent to an ICU if his condition is serious, or if it is less serious, he will be asked to come back once a week for follow-up checks. Depending on its performance, a subsidiary's ranking may change upon evaluation, and subsequently the decision rights that are delegated to it."

- When the parent company feels that the subsidiary is still not fully capable of handling important commercial or operational issues alone. This was the case with one company I talked to, who said they started to delegate decision rights to their subsidiary because they felt it now has sufficient experience and capability to handle its businesses alone. But if the parent's perception of its subsidiary's capabilities is inaccurate, large underestimation and undesirable intervention may damage incentives of the subsidiary.
- When the corporate head-office finds it necessary to act actively across the corporate group to achieve its strategic goals, regardless of the performance of its subsidiary. Actions may be geared towards speeding up transformation or optimizing activities to facilitate and maximize synergies. For example, Hitachi announced on July 1st 2013 to merge two of its subsidiaries — Hitachi Metals and Hitachi Cable — as part of Hitachi's restructuring to enhance synergies in its high-functional material business segment.
- When the parent company is highly dependent on the subsidiary's role, such that daily operation entails frequent parent–subsidiary communication, coordination, and at times interference. For example, MHI has around 11 business subsidiaries which have relatively more discretionary power than its hundreds of functional

subsidiaries in its core business of heavy industry, where decision making tends to be more centralized.

Although according to theory, actions of control and coordination may damage *ex-ante* incentives of the subsidiaries to invest in efforts, the case studies revealed that this does not necessarily have to be the case. Through effective and repeated coordination, the parent and its subsidiaries mutually agree on the boundary of actions, responsibilities and performance levels. When in doubt as to whether a certain issue should be handled alone or whether it should to be coordinated in advance, a subsidiary would consult its head-office counterpart. A parent company could also use *ex-post* intervention that is mutually agreed and hence acceptable to the subsidiary. Hitachi's flexible ranking system based on performance, as we saw earlier, is an example of such contingent control where interference occurs only when the subsidiary under-performs. The appropriate balance between delegation and intervention has to be worked out by the parent and the subsidiary, and there is no one-size fits all solution. From the case study, it can be observed that "mutual consent" is an important factor that reconciles incentive and intervention.

6.4.3 Managing Parent and Subsidiary Relationship

In Chapter 5, we looked at various aspects concerning parent–subsidiary relationships, in particular the existence of incompatible dual pressures, such as the need to differentiate in order to meet local market demands whilst also to integrate in order to reduce costs and attain economies of scale. We also looked at how perception gaps between the head-office and subsidiary concerning the subsidiary's role could generate conflicts that may be problematic, or quite the contrary, bring innovation and change.

In the case studies, I was rather surprised, therefore, that despite the many literatures on dual pressures and conflict, most of the companies that I have interviewed did not admit to having such conflict problems. This may be because Japanese culture encourages harmony, bottom-up coordination and mutual consent, and, therefore, conflicts are rare. Or it could be that admitting to having parent–subsidiary conflicts bear such a highly negative image that it is impermissible to say so. With the general non-disclosibility of problematic issues, and with hence rather limited information, I could only identify several factors that affect conflict and relationship between parent and subsidiary.

(a) The Stage of Business Development

Although institutional distance might exist between the parent head-office and its overseas subsidiary, conflict may not arise because both parties understand that major decisions has to be made at the home country head-office or district headquarter, and the subsidiary plays only a minor complementary role in providing local information that cannot be observed by the parent. However, at later stages of business development, when the subsidiary has more power to make decisions independently, conflict may arise between the subsidiary's pressures for localization, and the parent's pressure for overall optimization.

I should emphasise here that conflict is not necessarily undesirable. Conflict can highlight problems and decision trade-offs, and can offer opportunities for the company to make improvements. Seen in this light, very little conflict may be more worrisome than having conflicts if it implies weaknesses in identifying problems, and failure in utilizing local information.

(b) Subsidiary Type

A second factor that affects parent–subsidiary conflict concerns the type of subsidiary and hence the subsidiary's relationship with its parent company. In corporate groups that have many subsidiaries that run their own businesses such as Hitachi and Panasonic, there may be less conflict from dual pressures because subsidiaries have a high degree of autonomy and do not have to frequently consult or obtain approval from the corporate head-office. Performances are being monitored, and it is only when promises and budget plans are not fully kept that the head-office steps in to interfere. One manager described the situation as follows:

> "There are dual pressures, but it is up to the subsidiary's top management to decide how and to what extent the balance should be. This is fine because the subsidiary ultimately has to be responsible to its shareholder for its performance."

On the other hand, in corporate groups where subsidiaries are mainly production units, and where the parent depends on the subsidiary for the function it performs in the production value chain, there may be a stronger centralized control that could create conflict, especially when there are perception gaps concerning the role and capability of the subsidiary. For example, the parent may perceive and treat its subsidiary as a cost centre, while the subsidiary may wish to pursue more business with external clients as a profit centre.

(c) Clarity and Consistency regarding the Subsidiary's Role

A lack of clarity and consistency regarding the subsidiary's role may also create conflict, as the parent and subsidiary may form different expectations regarding the subsidiary's role. In the case study, for example, MHI stresses the importance of communicating the group's strategy to its subsidiaries and having the subsidiaries understand their individual roles within the corporate group. A manager at MHI describes the situation as follows:

> "There was, I think, a time in the past when we used to put pressure on our subsidiaries to purchase our products and to have them take on our redundant employees. Sometimes they were treated as merely one of many suppliers, and sometimes they were asked to be independent business entities, but suddenly when needed, they were asked to adhere to orders from the head-office or absorb effects of poor performances. The inconsistent and changing expectations bred frustration within subsidiaries and conflict with the parent company. But times have changed, and so has our policy towards our subsidiaries. Today, all our subsidiaries have a clear mission and role identity within the corporate group as you can see in the MHI Group brochure. Our emphasis now is not so much on having our subsidiaries expand their businesses with external clients individually, but more on focusing internally on how we can enhance synergy in our core businesses by mobilizing our resources and capabilities."

(d) Changes in Technology and Business Environment

The case study also revealed that changes in technology and business environment affect parent–subsidiary relationship. For example, in the case of Nihon Yusen (NYK), changes in industry technology and the environment of its container liner business greatly affected transactions between NYK and its subsidiary. A manager at Nihon Yusen described the situation as follows:

"In the past, our liner business division would fill their cargo space by selling to large corporate clients like Panasonic and Toyota. But as ocean liners get bigger with the improvement of technology such that we now own ships that carry over 10,000 TEUs, it becomes very hard for us, even with alliances, to fill the spaces solely by our own effort. This means risks are much higher, and we don't afford to carry cargo just one way and then carry back empty containers. Not only is the market commoditized, demand is also highly volatile, such that we need to hedge against low demand and low prices. We, therefore, sell part of our space at cheap rates to our logistics subsidiaries that operate NVOCC (Non Vessel Operator Cargo Carrier) business, and they in return guarantee filling those spaces. But this is no cosy parent-subsidiary arrangement. Yusen Logistics is not obliged to use NYK liners. In fact it purchases space based on the most favourable terms available in the market, so it may or may not be NYK."

Technology and business conditions demand that even with intra-group transactions, both the parent company's liner business and the subsidiary's logistics business have to be at least as competitive as the market. Under such conditions, there is no room for cosy mutual dependency, and the parent–subsidiary relationship moves towards a more market like type of relationship.

With a shrinking domestic market, many corporations are seeking growth opportunities abroad. A manager of a large corporate group commented that as his company became more globalized, and expanded businesses abroad and recruited talent from abroad to work in both its Japan head-office and overseas subsidiaries, the company needed to devise new management systems to cope with the changing organization. Many implicit rules, norms and role expectations which were previously shared and understood by subsidiaries, had to be made more explicit because employees now came from different cultural backgrounds.

(e) Bridge Between Parent and Subsidiary

In Chapter 5, we looked at the issue of knowledge diffusion, and discussed how multiple community membership within a corporate group can bridge structural holes in social networks and help the brokering of collective knowledge. The coordination and control systems that the case study firms use serve as brokering functions that allow diffusion of knowledge between the parent and its subsidiaries. The stress on mutual acceptance allows both the parent and the subsidiary to make explicit issues that require coordination, and staffs who are seconded or transferred act as mediators that facilitate the flow of information and knowledge.

For example, in the case of Japan Airlines, in which the head-office counter-part department works closely with the company's IT subsidiary, mutual coordination creates value because the counter-part department has specialized knowledge about its business requirements whilst the IT subsidiary has specialized knowledge in IT, including the know-how that is accumulated through external transactions that can be leveraged by the corporate group to craft solutions. Coordination distributes cognition that helps the parent and the subsidiary to co-produce value.

6.4.4 Norms and Self-Enforcing Mechanisms

So far in this section, we have looked at formal coordination and delegation systems that corporate groups use to manage their subsidiaries. In this sub-section, we shall discuss about informal rules and norms that companies use to facilitate interaction and coordination.

How do firms ensure that their many divisions and subsidiaries follow corporate policies and rules in practice? A corporate headquarter may prescribe many rules and expect all its employees across the whole corporate group to follow them. But if the employees do not know which policy or rule to refer to before they act, or if they fail to notice and act upon the latest revised rule, or if shared meaning of the rules does not exist, then it is likely that there will be many occurrences of non-compliance. This is why one firm I talked to said they have been putting extra efforts in structuring rules for easy reference, listing up rules that are likely to be required for each job function, and holding regular meetings to brief subsidiaries on additions and changes to corporate rules and regulations. A company may also systematically distribute cognitions amongst members through routines where head-office departments and subsidiaries coordinate and share knowledge.

In addition to formal rules, informal rules and norms also play an important part in facilitating shared general understanding that essentially makes business corporations self-governing. A manager at Panasonic described their norm as follows:

> "We at Panasonic place great emphasis on our management philosophy. The seven beliefs, established by our founder Konosuke Matsushita, are read aloud every day in morning assemblies, they are quoted and used frequently in meetings, and they are a subject at study meetings and seminars. As a result of this emphasis and routine usage, the Panasonic management philosophy is very much shared amongst employees within the group."

The case of Japan Airlines provides a good example of active use of self-enforcement. Japan Airlines (hereafter referred to as JAL) has what is called the JAL Philosophy, which was instituted in January 2011 and is said to have played a vital role in the company's restructuring after bankruptcy. JAL places this Philosophy alongside its performance management systems as core components of their management. All employees are handed a booklet of 125 pages, in which the 40 articles of JAL Philosophy are printed. It begins with the Formula for Success, which reads:

Result of Life and Work = Attitude × Effort × Ability

The formula stresses having a right attitude, because if it is negative, the outcomes will always be negative even with the brightest talent. Plugging in a −100 or a +100 to the formula makes a great difference to the outcome.

Unlike a couple of overarching value proposals or identity statements used in some corporate philosophies to empower employees to make decisions without having to rely on rules and manuals that are in nature never complete, the 40 articles of JAL Philosophy prompt employees to evaluate an issue from multiple angles, by referring to the articles that are related to the issue at hand. In order to apply the Philosophy, it has to be studied repeatedly so that all members of the group would share a common language, quote and draw insights from the Philosophy, and agree on a just way of handling matters.

Prescribed norms and values change from merely beautifully crafted words to embedded norms and values only when they are used regularly. Through regular usage, they become part of the language and part of the way in which employees frame and view issues. Many companies that I have talked to, appear to share this view on frequent usage. Commitment by top management is another crucial factor that leads to successful adoption and hence frequent usage of prescribed norms. In Japan Airlines, philosophy study sessions started from the very top, and moved down the hierarchy, such that today, there are study sessions, formal and informal, in nearly all departments. Executive officers often quote words from the JAL Philosophy in speeches, messages and documents that are directed to employees, so that frequent usage could prompt awareness.

In my case interview with JAL Infotec (hereafter referred to as JIT), an IT subsidiary of JAL, I was struck first by the enthusiasm the manager displayed towards the JAL Philosophy, and then by the impact the Philosophy had on its parent–subsidiary relationship. Since its introduction, JAL has been organizing rounds of regular group-wide study sessions in various regions where staffs from head-office and subsidiaries gather to study, discuss and share views concerning the JAL Philosophy. In addition to these formal sessions, many staff initiated study groups have sprung up across the company in many areas, one of which is organized by staff of JIT.

The effects are quite astonishing. For example, although the origins might have existed earlier, the adoption of internal control systems in JIT was far from ceremonial. The JAL Philosophy helped spread the awareness of internal control, and as a manager in JIT described, it became very much a habit.

"Take for example something as simple as locking your desk drawer after work. Our staff would feel very uncomfortable if they think they might have forgotten to do so. He or she will have this insecure feeling that feels like driving a car without putting on a seatbelt or like riding a motorcycle without a helmet."

JIT developed its own internal control systems and study program, which proved to be so well worked out that in just one year, that over a hundred JAL head-office personnel, from senior directors to managers, have attended JIT's study programme. This served as a good example of knowledge and best practices flowing from the subsidiary to the parent company.

Regarding internal control in JIT, rules are not seen merely as a long list of things that need to be observed, but as a reason for doing things the way they are intended to be done. They are not seen as wearisome extra work, but as an accepted way of mitigating risks and protecting the company and its employees.

In addition to facilitating the adoption of rules, best practices and knowledge between parent and subsidiary, the JAL Philosophy also changed the relationship between JAL and JIT. In one of their business negotiation processes, JAL did not exert control power over JIT although it could have chosen to do so. Rather the process was based on what is deemed proper through the lens of the JAL Philosophy. In demanding flexibility, JAL could have wanted JIT to perform a system fix by just placing an order over the phone or by email, whilst leaving the contract terms and red tape to be sorted out later. However, such a practice would go against JIT's internal control rules that require performing tasks only after having received a valid order contract. When JAL's procurement department and JIT discussed over this issue, both parties agreed on what is just and proper based on their shared understanding derived from the JAL Philosophy.

As the above example shows, although rules and norms may be seen as constraining, they are also enabling because rules can aid individual's knowledge of how others are likely to play, thus helping them play effectively. Rules become self-enforcing when employees do not have the incentive to play otherwise. They also help facilitate diffusion of knowledge and best practices both from parent to subsidiary, as well as from subsidiary to parent.

Another example can be seen in what I have described earlier about Hitachi's delegation of decision rights to its subsidiaries that is contingent upon each subsidiary's performance. Here too, repeated interaction makes the system self-enforcing as each subsidiary acquires a cognitive frame as to how to play — perform well and more autonomy will be granted, perform poorly and autonomy will be reduced. This kind of shared understanding is important because it facilitates mutual consent, which forms the basis of the system of balancing control and delegation that many Japanese companies use.

6.5 A SUMMARY OF ACADEMIC AND PRACTITIONER'S KNOWLEDGE

Table 10 summarizes the main academic knowledge and practitioner's knowledge discussed in this chapter. Although the practitioner's knowledge are based mainly on the case study of five large corporate groups, they are contents-wise not highly firm specific, and could, therefore, to a large extent be generalizable to other large Japanese corporate groups.

Table 10: Combining academic knowledge with practitioner's knowledge

	Academic Knowledge	Practitioner's Knowledge
Firm Boundary	**Transaction Cost Theory/Incentive Theory/Property Rights Approach** Use of subsidiaries balance high internal transaction costs that arise from excessive control, and high external transaction costs that arise from using the market. Reduction of excessive control also solves the incentive problem where expectation of *ex-post* intervention could curb incentives to invest in efforts *ex-ante*. Firms choose to own subsidiary and have control over residual rights when there is uncertainty, and when investments bring residual returns, especially when owning complementary assets create value. Use of subsidiaries also balances control when there are high costs involved in allocating control rights exclusively to one party. **Resourced Based View** Tacit knowledge makes trading of capabilities difficult, and this may determine the group boundary because cognitive constraints may increase cost of integrating across diverse external capabilities.	**Balancing Centripetal and Centrifugal Forces** Japanese corporate groups aim to maintain a balance between centrifugal and centripetal forces. Incentives are maintained because of coordination systems that emphasise mutual agreement between parent and subsidiary. The economic rational of using subsidiaries is not limited to balancing transaction costs but includes the ability to choose from a wider range of strategic options amongst using in-house, subsidiary, and market. *Ex-post* **Lock-in of Group Boundary** After a subsidiary has been established, other make or buy criteria such as utilization exist. High switching costs and biases that justify using subsidiary over market may also prolong lock-in, and may result in internal transaction costs outweighing external transaction costs. Lock-in often depends on the type of subsidiary and its relationship with the parent company. **Knowledge Defines the Group Boundary** High cost of integrating knowledge and high switching cost may create a lock-in situation where a firm will not want to alter or change players of the existing game even when performances are sub-optimal, and internal costs have become high.

(Continued)

Table 10: (*Continued*)

	Academic Knowledge	Practitioner's Knowledge
Firm Boundary	**Contingency Theory** There is no best way to organize a corporation, and that the optimal course of action is contingent upon the company's internal and external environment. Empirical studies show, for example, that diversification drives companies to delegate more decision rights to subsidiaries.	The case study identified strategic necessities for using subsidiaries to respond to changes in environment. (a) Integrate vertically when production inputs cannot be procured from the market. (b) Use subsidiaries in order to comply with legal requirements. (c) Use subsidiaries to change existing competitive environment. (d) Use subsidiaries to develop business opportunities. (e) Respond to host country demands. (f) Tailor offering to better meet customer demand. (g) Enter or expand penetration into markets that have growth potential. (h) To access or have ownership over scarce resources. (i) Develop synergies, acquire competencies.
Group Management	**Vertical and Horizontal Coordination** Managers and workers who have proper understanding of central management instructions, adjust those instructions using the local information that they perfectly observe. Benefits of coordination have to outweigh communication costs. **Decentralization and Delegation of Decision Rights** Possibility of designing a decentralized hierarchy that could achieve optimal centralized outcomes. Select appropriate level of decentralization based on the costs and benefits of delegation. Costs: Incentive cost, control loss and power abuse. Benefits: Access to local information, better and quicker decision-making.	**Coordination Systems** Corporate groups have multiple coordination systems that are used effectively alongside decentralization and delegation systems. (a) Counterpart head-office department (b) Group management department (c) Functional meetings (d) Personnel rotations, secondments and transfers Effectiveness of coordination system is monitored through performance checks.

Group Management

Incentive Theory

Use subsidiaries to signal commitment by the parent company not to interfere *ex-post* such that the subsidiaries and their business divisions will have the incentive to invest in firm specific efforts

Parent–Subsidiary Relationship

Dual pressures that could lead to conflict. Normative integration through socialization could reduce conflict. Agency problems may arise such that subsidiaries may pursue interests that diverge from the corporate group's goals. This can be reduced by monitoring and by designing incentive compatible contracts.

Subsidiaries may play mixed motive games that pursue local interests while share interest in the corporate group's prosperity.

Evolutionary games allow players to learn and change strategy over time.

Perception gaps concerning the subsidiary's role may generate different expectations and thus conflict.

Self-Enforcing Mechanisms

Rules are norms may be seen as constraining, but they are also enabling because rules can aid individual's knowledge of how other are likely to play, and thus help them play effectively.

Delegation Systems

Delegation used with intervention. Intervention is contingent upon performance or is mutually agreed, such that subsidiary incentives are not damaged.

Parent–Subsidiary Conflict

(a) Stage of business development

Conflict is less at early phase of business when the parent makes all major decisions, while the subsidiary plays only a minor complementary role. But conflict increases later when the subsidiary has the power to press for interests that differ from that of the parent.

(b) Type of Subsidiary

Conflict may arise when the parent and subsidiary have different interests, and when there are perception gaps regarding the subsidiary's role.

(c) Clarity and Consistency

Lack of clarity and consistency regarding the subsidiary's role could cause case conflict

Changes in industry technology and business environment also alter parent and subsidiary relationship, and may create tension.

Rules and Norms

Frequent usage and commitment by top management are crucial in embedding norms.

Norms facilitate dissemination of knowledge and best practices between parent and subsidiary, and facilitate coordinated action.

Chapter 7

CLASSIFICATION OF DIFFERENT TYPES OF SUBSIDIARIES

In the process of mapping academic theories and literatures against practices that are observed in the cases, I became acutely aware of the situation where the extent to which theories and practice concur varies depending on the type of subsidiary and its corresponding parent–subsidiary relationship.

For example, if we say that the rationale of using subsidiaries is to balance internal and external transaction costs, as theory posits, we might ask whether this rationale holds for all different kinds of subsidiaries. And we may argue that if a subsidiary supplies goods or services that form the core competencies of its parent company, then the relationship may require more control than a subsidiary that is spun-off as an individual business with discretion over its own business. Hence excessive control could be regarded as more incentive damaging if the subsidiary is an independent business rather than a production unit that requires close coordination with the parent company.

In order to evaluate the extent to which practice conforms to theory — such as the cost balance rationale — it is useful to identify and classify the different types of parent–subsidiary relationships that exist, and treat them separately rather than generalizing them as something that is homogeneous. Part of the purpose of this book, therefore, is to identify and distinguish different types of parent and subsidiary relationships, and to link the typology to academic theories by mapping out how theory holds for each type of subsidiary. I hope this would further initiate theoretical and empirical developments that would deepen our understanding of this topic.

7.1 TYPOLOGY OF SUBSIDIARIES

Before I discuss the classification of subsidiaries based on my case study results, I find it appropriate at this point to briefly go through some of the major literature on the classification of subsidiaries. Enright and Subramanian (2012) offered an activity-based typology approach, in which they posited that not only is the presence or absence of a particular activity comparatively easier to measure, it also provides a more reliable way to study subsidiary roles. Results of their empirical study of 1,100 U.S., European and Japanese firms support a four-part typology of subsidiary roles: management and development, full functional subsidiaries, production bases, sales and service subsidiaries. This typology helps us to identify, for example, that a significant number of subsidiaries are production bases, whilst a relatively low number of subsidiaries are given the role of management and development.

Birkinshaw (1995, 2005), on the other hand, described the subsidiary roles as 'Specialized Contributor' and 'World Mandate'. The former type performs a limited number of functions in the value chain and requires a high degree of control by the parent for integration and coordination purposes. The latter type holds regional or world-wide responsibility for the whole of the product and performs most of the activities in the value chain. Birkinshaw's classification of subsidiaries is based on the relative strength of the subsidiary's internal competitive arena within the MNC and external competitive arena. His work hypothesized and found support that the more focused the subsidiary is on its external competitive arena, the greater its degree of entrepreneurship. He argued that the more internally focused the subsidiary is, the more strategic decision making are taken out of the subsidiary's hands and held at a corporate level. In dual-focused environments, it depends on whether or not the internal or external pressures dominate.

Birkinshaw, together with Frost and Ensign (2002) also hypothesized and found support that a subsidiary can become a centre of excellence through conditions of the subsidiary's local environment, such as links to external sources of competencies, and relationships with other parts of the corporate group, such as autonomy of the subsidiary. A parent company, on the other hand, can provide intangible assets such as skills, knowledge, and expertise, as well as tangible assets such as investment capital, that is needed by the subsidiary to develop capabilities that would lead to competitive advantage. This idea of centre of excellence has immense implications in Japan where subsidiaries essentially make up a corporate group, such that the extent to which subsidiaries are capable of developing competencies is of vital importance to both the subsidiary itself and the corporate group as a whole.

Taking a different approach, Ambos and Schlegelmilch (2007) did not just look at the types of subsidiaries, but also hypothesized that the headquarters' ability to control its subsidiaries is contingent on the relative resource power as well as the task context of the subsidiary, which in his study was an overseas R&D unit. They study found support for their hypothesis that headquarters will respond to increasing interdependencies with an increase in centralization, formalization and socialization. Their results also showed that relative to subsidiaries that only need to adapt products to local markets, subsidiaries that exploit the firm's competencies and create new competencies will experience higher levels of centralization.

Practitioners also have their classification. In Japan, from the case studies and well as from many business literatures, the categorization that is most commonly used is a general distinction between what is referred to as a functional subsidiary (*kinou kogaisha*) and a business subsidiary (*jigyou kogaisha*). However, there does not appear to be any formal definition regarding the two types of subsidiaries, and meanings can vary. In some companies, a functional subsidiary means a subsidiary that specializes in corporate functions such as accounting and IT, while in other companies the definition incudes hived-off manufacturing bases. In some companies "business" means profit centres and "functional" means cost centres, while in some companies "functional" can be both profit and cost centres at the same time. Nonetheless, a common general description would be as follows. A functional subsidiary is a subsidiary that performs specific functions within the value chain of the corporate group. Such a subsidiary is often regarded as a cost centre, and is, therefore, expected to provide the core businesses with quality and cost for specified goods and services. A business subsidiary, on the other hand, is a subsidiary that contributes to the group consolidated revenue through its own business activities, and is regarded as a profit centre. There are also subsidiaries that perform certain functions for the parent company whilst also have their own external clients, and are hence both cost and profit centres. Simple as this classification of business and functional may appear, it does reveal to some extent the interdependency between the parent and the subsidiary.

The magazine *Business Research* (2011, 3–4) published a report based on information of 122 functional subsidiaries of 11 corporate groups. The report described the characteristics of functional subsidiaries as follows:

- 89 functions were identified and categorized, including management and maintenance of real estate and facilities, sales, HR (salary, welfare and training), information systems, R&D, support functions, production and logistics.
- In most cases, functional subsidiaries were established a result of hived off functions that were previously performed by the parent company. The main reasons for establishing such subsidiaries were to reduce costs (81% of the 89 functions) and to improve efficiency and effectiveness on areas that require specialized skills (62%). Cost reduction was achieved through lowering wages (60%), consolidating common functions (46%), and down-sizing headquarter (43%).
- Most of the functional subsidiaries are 100% owned by the parent company.

- Although size and revenue of the subsidiaries vary, over 60% of the functional subsidiaries transact mainly with firms within their own corporate group. (Over 80% of trading partners are internal). These subsidiaries depend very much on their parent for sales revenue.

Much of the material from my case studies agree with the above mentioned academic and practitioner findings, that subsidiaries perform different activities, that the power of subsidiaries are often derived from the dependency the parent and other subsidiaries have on them, and that the degree of centralization and power delegation often depends on the strategic importance of the subsidiary concerned. But I hope to add value to existing knowledge in two ways.

Firstly, I hope to create a typology that describes the different parent and subsidiary interdependencies that exist. Although in existing literatures, the responsibility-based classification into regional or world-wide, local adaptors or international adaptors highlight the strategic importance of the subsidiaries that are being classified, and hence to certain degrees their level of controls by the corporate headquarters, the classifications tell rather little about the interdependency which is often needed to discern control and coordination issues. For example, although an independent profit generating subsidiary is strategically important, just as a subsidiary that supplies core manufacturing components to the corporation's value chain is strategically important, the former may require more decentralization whereas the latter may require more centralization. Classifying both as strategically important risks mixing two essentially different subsidiary types into one, when in reality, parent and subsidiary interactions are very different. A typology based on interdependency would provide a practical frame to analyze different parent and subsidiary relationships. Secondly, I hope to go beyond developing a typology, to using it as a tool to evaluate how theories apply differently to different types of subsidiaries. From a practitioner's perspective this would provide useful insights that could help a corporate group design control and coordination mechanisms that best suit each subsidiary type.

7.1.1 A Four Part Classification of Subsidiaries based on Interdependency

Through a series of interviews with five large corporate groups, namely Hitachi, Panasonic, Nihon Yusen, Japan Airlines and Mitsubishi Heavy Industry, conducted between September 2012 and January 2013, in which I sought to understand why corporations need subsidiaries and how they manage them, I asked the case study companies how they classify their subsidiaries. Although there was no uniform answer from the interviews with regards to the classification of subsidiaries, I observed firstly that there is a dependency relationship between the parent and its subsidiary which may be mutual or unilateral. Unilateral in that a parent may depend on the subsidiary's output, or vice versa, and mutually dependant when both the parent and the subsidiary depend on each other. I also observed that both the parent and subsidiary may each trade either internally within the group, externally with outside clients, or both internally and externally. Based on these observations, I constructed a matric as shown in Figure 17, which depicts four distinct types of parent and subsidiary relationships.

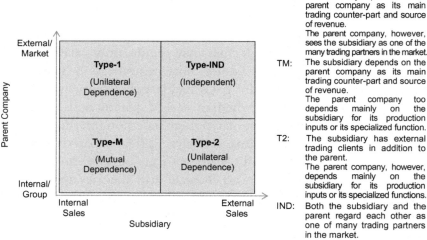

Figure 17:   Four types of subsidiaries

The vertical axis represents the parent company's range of choices between external and internal transaction such as procurement of inputs, while the horizontal axis represents the subsidiary's range of choices between external and internal transaction such as sales of outputs. The four part matrix represents four possible types of transaction relationship between the parent and its subsidiary, taking into account the perspective of both the parent company and the subsidiary company concerned.

To verify if this classification is valid for other corporate groups, I held further discussions with nine other corporate groups between June 2013 and September 2013 through four sessions of group study.[5] All nine corporate groups agreed that this matrix serves as a good representation for classifying their subsidiaries. Using this classification revealed that with these corporate groups, on average 5% of the subsidiaries fall into Type 1, a majority of 70% fall into Type M, 7% fall into Type IND, and 18% fall into Type 2. I will now describe each of the four different types of parent–subsidiary relationship and discuss the extent to which theory — in particular the cost balance rationale of having subsidiaries — holds.

7.2 DISCUSSION: LINKING TYPOLOGY OF SUBSIDIARY TO THEORY

Type 1: Unilateral Dependence

A subsidiary belonging to this type sells its goods and services chiefly to its parent company. The subsidiary usually has expertise in one area that contributes to a larger product or service value chain. The parent company, however, regards the subsidiary as one of many suppliers in the market, and may choose to switch to other suppliers in the market when conditions are favourable. The subsidiary which has weak bargaining power when negotiating with its parent, and is susceptible to

---

[5] The discussions were organized by the Business Research Institute, where in the study group for parent and subsidiary transactions, the following ten corporate groups participated. They are namely, Mitsui Chemicals, Kewpie, Kawasaki Heavy Industries, Citizen Holdings, Sompo Japan Insurance, JTB, Japan Airlines, Mitsubishi Gas Chemical, Mitsui Chemicals, Nippon Steel & Sumitomo Metal.`

losses should its parent decide to procure from elsewhere, strives to be at least as competitive as the market in order to win orders. The parent company may abuse its power to demand flexibility and low costs such that all profits are absorbed and taken away by the parent. Under such circumstances, the subsidiary may lose incentive to be entrepreneurial.

A frequently asked question is whether a subsidiary should earn profits from its parent company? From my interviews, there appears to be mixed views concerning what a subsidiary ought to be in the first place. Some firms argue that the purpose of a subsidiary, being part of the production value chain, is primarily to supply specified goods or services at the lowest possible cost and specified quality. Milking profit from the parent company is, therefore, deemed undesirable and should, therefore, be checked. On the other hand, there are also firms that argue that profit is a necessary incentive that allows subsidiaries to be entrepreneurial, such that they would seek to make continuous improvements that in the end would benefit both the subsidiary and the parent company. In other words a win-win approach rather than an exploitative approach to managing functional subsidiaries is deemed appropriate.

Indeed, Sonoda (2004) explained that functional subsidiaries have in them embedded mechanisms that inhibit growth. The more a subsidiary reduces its costs, the lesser will the price be that it charges its parent, and hence the lesser will its revenue become. Remuneration-linked reward raises labour cost and is, therefore, hard to implement because lowering labour cost is often the prime purpose of having the functional subsidiary in the first place. Cost reduction often entails quality trade-offs, such that with the emphasis placed on cost, the subsidiary may withhold quality improvements despite having the capability to do so. Sonoda, therefore, proposed the use of non-financial appraisal systems such as the balanced score card as a means to manage both cost and quality, as well as to allow the subsidiary communicate the non-financial benefits it delivers to the corporate group. The management issue is not one of deciding between exploitation and entrepreneurialism, but one of striking a good balance that will neither curb incentives of the subsidiary nor allow production cost and quality go unchecked.

The Type-1 subsidiary appears puzzling as we may wonder why a company would need a Type-1 subsidiary when it is possible and sometimes more feasible for the parent company to procure from the market. In my field research, I identified two plausible explanations. In the case of company A, a Type-M subsidiary was established to lower production costs, but years later, with the pressing need to improve international competitiveness, the subsidiary was redefined as Type-1 so as to expose it to pseudo external competition.

Type-1 can also be the result of a lock-in situation. When prompted with lowering external transaction costs a parent may gradually shift towards external sources instead of using the subsidiary. But then in many cases, at least in the short term, the parent company is also locked into using the subsidiary. As a manager in company B describes, "Once you have a subsidiary, which in our case is a manufacturing plant, you cannot just simply switch to an outside supplier because you also need to consider the subsidiary's utilization rate and profits as well." There are other reasons as well, such as retaining a competence that may be required at a later phase of a strategic plan. A manager in company C describes, "Although we often use external suppliers, we also maintain a subsidiary as a competence we would like to have in our corporate portfolio."

It is also worth noting, as seen from the above examples that a subsidiary type is not static and subsidiaries can move from one type to another. If indeed a Type-1 subsidiary no longer creates value, then the corporate head office might decide to divest it or shift it to another more suitable category, such as from Type-1 to Type IND, though such a move may be perilous if the subsidiary does not have the competencies that are needed to compete externally.

Whether maintaining a certain subsidiary type can be accounted for by cost balance depends on how much control is needed. For a Type-1 subsidiary, control and coordination may not be so much of an issue since the parent is not dependent on the subsidiary for its output. The rationale for assigning a Type-1 subsidiary would likely to be more on improving production efficiency by introducing some form of competition, rather than to balance internal and external transaction costs.

Type M: Mutual Dependence

A subsidiary belonging to this type sells its goods and services mainly to its parent company. The parent company too is highly dependent on the goods and services its subsidiary provides, and may often exert control over decision making even on matters concerning day-to-day operation. Many such subsidiaries are created with the purpose of specializing in a particular activity that is part of the company's production value chain. One of the chief reasons for doing so, according to Ito (2004), is to reduce labour cost, and thereby production cost in order to be cost competitive. However, it should be noted that although a company could take advantage of cheap labour costs provided by its first, second and subsequent tiers of subsidiaries, these benefits could be depleted if the parent–subsidiary production setting breeds inefficiencies that could outweigh cost benefits.

Dependency is often inevitable when there are no other suppliers in the market that can substitute the functions performed by the subsidiary, and when the parent worries that proprietary technology may be copied and imitated when external suppliers are used. Another form of dependency that is prevalent in many Japanese corporate groups can be found in the parent company's need to fulfil its lifetime employment commitments by having its subsidiaries hire the parent company's surplus labour. Such HR practices may be beneficial if the transferred employees carry and transfer skills that are useful to the subsidiary. But if their skills do not fit, such practices may destroy rather than create value.

One may intuitively think that because of mutual dependency, interests of the parent and subsidiary are aligned centripetally. But it is possible that without conflict, mutual dependency and cosy parent–subsidiary relationships, denoted by the Japanese term "*nareai*", could breed inefficiencies and creates taken-for-granted black boxes, such that high costs are left unquestioned because they are seen as necessary production costs by the subsidiary, or because there is little incentive to check and revise trading terms with its subsidiaries. A manager of a subsidiary company once said to me, "Our former parent company essentially paid whatever price we charged them because there was this mind-set that with intra-group transactions, cash merely flows within the group and is fine because there is no real cash outflow. Trading terms however became much more severe after our company was taken over in an M&A and ceased to be that firm's subsidiary." A manager of another subsidiary said, "Because there is no market price for the firm-specific goods and services that we supply to our parent company, the revenue we receive is whatever our cost of production is plus a certain profit mark-up." The parent company's inability to identify suitable benchmarks for making cost and quality comparisons, may also lead to a failure in detecting and controlling inefficiencies for prolonged periods. Another often mentioned justification for high costs is that the subsidiary performs such highly firm-specific functions that its assumed superior quality and greater flexibility are sufficient to justify a premium price.

The subsidiary, in having no other source of revenue other than that from its parent company, and seeing also that its parent has no other alternative, may seek to milk profits from the parent company. This is not to say that all Type-M subsidiaries are problematic. But because many subsidiaries appear to fall within this category (70% of subsidiaries from the case study firms), caution is needed to make sure that routinized parent–subsidiary transactions do not create organizational inertia and excessive rigidity in the corporate group boundary. It is also important to balance firm specific production knowledge with new technology that may not be accessible within the corporate group.

The control side of the cost balance is not necessarily a big issue to a Type-M subsidiary because the parent company's dependency on its subsidiary usually entails some form of control and coordination at the strategic as well as operational level. But still one may worry whether control would damage incentives and reduce productivity. If, as the incentive theory suggests, subsidiaries are used as a means of signalling commitment by the parent company not to interfere *ex-post*, and by doing so enhance *ex-ante* incentives of business units to invest in firm specific efforts, then wouldn't control curb incentives and defeat the purpose of having subsidiaries? This could be the case when control is excessive, but although companies often apply centripetal forces to balance centrifugal forces so as to ensure that the group's overall strategic goals can be met, it appears that incentives are generally maintained because of an emphasis on mutual agreement between the parent and its subsidiary as discussed previously in Chapter 5. Hence, although subsidiaries may be used as a means to balance excessive control as theory suggests, it is also the case that control and coordination systems are used to help align incentives and transfer tacit knowledge.

For example, the counterpart or managing department performs what Owan and Kato (2008) describe as hybrid coordination because it aggregates local information of the subsidiaries that it oversees, and coordinates activities to ensure that they are aligned with vertical controls and strategy execution. In my field research, managers explained that through effective coordination, the parent company and subsidiary often agree on a set of actions or responsibilities and performance level that the parent company is comfortable with, such that the subsidiary can have discretion over delegated decision making. The effectiveness of control and coordination would depend on whether they produce positive conflict and hence improvement rather than routinized relationship that creates inertia.

Type 2: Unilateral Dependence

A subsidiary belonging to this type sells its goods and services mainly to external clients in addition to its parent company. It is dual-focused in that it has to meet not only demands from its parent company but also business requirements of its external clients. The parent company, which is highly dependent on its subsidiary's output, may exert control over its subsidiary, and conflict of interest may give rise to tension between the parent company and subsidiary. For example, a subsidiary may wish to mobilize its resources to expand sales production outside the corporate group, but its parent company may want the subsidiary to reduce its external sales and focus its limited resources on internal supply chain. Or for example, a subsidiary may be expected by its parent company to provide expert knowledge on existing legacy systems technologies, but the subsidiary also needs to upgrade its knowledge base that is often developed and acquired externally, without which the subsidiary would risk having a limited life span.

By having a subsidiary sway more towards external sales, both the parent company and the subsidiary could benefit from economies of scope and scale, if the subsidiary could reduce its marginal cost of production by producing more as a result of having many external clients. The subsidiary is also freed from the constraint of production not exceeding the production and marketing capacity of its parent company. Participation in the market will also force the subsidiary to be more competitive in quality and price, and the parent company may benefit from such external governance and from leveraging capabilities of the subsidiary.

In Japan, many corporations established IT subsidiaries in the 1980s, and many such subsidiaries, including several of the companies researched in this study, have subsequently expanded into providing services to external clients in addition to its functional role within the corporate group. In terms of the matrix in Figure 17, there was shift from Type-M to Type-2. In the post-bubble period of the 1990s, many IT subsidiaries, despite being recognized as strategically important, were pressed by their parent companies to cut costs. Because the conflicting goals of being a cost centre as well as a profit centre were incompatible, many subsidiaries found it hard to establish its long term goals and motivate its employees. According to Kagotani (2007), only a small number of Japanese IT subsidiaries in the 1980s succeeded in becoming profitable profit centres. From the late 1990s onwards, many IT subsidiaries had to withdraw from external sales and refocus on being cost centres, in other words shift from Type-2 to Type-M.

As the above example shows, the strategic role of subsidiaries and the amount of interference and control by the parent company can change over time, and it is not seldom that activities of subsidiaries are controlled for the sake of overall optimality. Many journalistic articles argue that the shedding of market share by Japanese electronics manufacturers to other Asian competitors can be attributed to Japan's rigid *jimaeshugi* or vertical integration, where subsidiaries often have to focus on supplying to their parent companies at the expense of propitious external businesses. This can be damaging to both the parent company, which misses to utilize fabless EMS to cut costs and to reach volume and market swiftly, and the subsidiary, which fails to develop its potential by specializing only on what it does best.

Because of severe dual pressures that a Type-2 subsidiary often faces, careful coordination and control is required so as not to curb the subsidiary's entrepreneurial incentives, whilst making sure at the same time that firm specific investments needed for the parent company's business is also maintained. Managers are often transferred or seconded to such subsidiaries to act as effective coordinators and mediators. In this type of subsidiary, one would expect the balance of control to be contingent on whether there are conflicting interests. In the absence of such conflict, more discretion will be given to the subsidiary, while in the event of conflict the parent may need to exert more direct control.

Independent Type (IND)

A subsidiary belonging to this type sells its goods and services mainly to its external clients. The subsidiary sees its parent company as just one of many clients in the market. The parent company is not dependent on the subsidiary's function, and sees it as an individual revenue generating business within the corporate group's portfolio.

A subsidiary may initially be established as a purely functional one, performing specific functions within the production value chain of the core business, such as manufacturing a certain component or performing logistic functions that support the corporate group's supply chain. As the subsidiary gains experience and expertise in servicing its parent company, it gradually develops competencies that could be applied to other production settings with external clients. By participating in the market and being exposed to competition, the subsidiary may further grow to excel in what it does best, such that it becomes increasingly an attractive supplier to both its parent company as well as other external clients. The subsidiary and consequently the parent may benefit from economies of scale and scope as larger production output reduces cost per unit. The subsidiary may eventually become a core business segment within the corporate group, and make substantial contributions to consolidate revenue. Indeed, this was the path Hitachi Transport System took to become a successful type IND subsidiary and an industry leader.

A Type-IND subsidiary may have very little transaction with the parent company or other companies within the corporate group, and, therefore, the cost balance consideration is less relevant here because the parent company need not worry transaction cost trade-offs. The parent company may be more concerned with the subsidiary's financial results and contribution to the corporate group's business portfolio, and may exert control when performance drops. One of my case study companies ranks its subsidiaries based on performance evaluation, and delegate decision right based such ranking, such that better performing subsidiaries are granted more discretion over decision making and hence more incentives to perform well.

In modularized industries where horizontal specialization has a good strategic fit, spinning off specialized subsidiaries into Type-IND firms may appear to be an attractive option. However, excessive control from the parent company may inhibit such growth, especially when the parent company is not familiar with the subsidiary's business, or when intervention slows down decision making. In such instances, measures are needed to restrict control, and *ex-post* monitoring rather than *ex-ante* intervention may be a more suitable form of governance.

7.3 MAPPING THEORY AND PRACTICE TO EACH SUBSIDIARY TYPE

Having described the four part classification of subsidiaries, and having discussed in some detail the extent to which the theory of balancing internal and external transaction costs holds for each subsidiary type, I will now briefly describe how other theories that have been mentioned so far in this book can be mapped against each subsidiary type (see Table 11). This, I hope, will illustrate how the typology can be used for analyzing how theories work differently under different parent–subsidiary settings.

Table 11: Mapping academic and practitioner's knowledge to subsidiary type

Academic and Practitioner's Knowledge	Types of Subsidiary
Transaction Cost Theory and Property Rights Approach	Different types of subsidiaries face different balance issues, such that control and coordination do not necessarily entail trade-offs in productivity.
Use subsidiaries to (1) balance high internal transaction costs that arise from excessive control that reduces productivity, and high external transaction costs that arise from using the market, and (2) balance control when there are high costs to allocating control rights exclusively to one party.	[Type 1 Subsidiary]
	Cherry pick favourable price and quality between the subsidiary and market whilst maintaining acceptable utilization rate of the subsidiary.
	[Type M Subsidiary]
	Balance between firm specific production knowledge and the acquisition of knowledge and new technology which may not be accessible inside the corporate group.
	Balance mutual dependency with appropriate monitoring to root out inefficiencies and inertia.
	[Type 2 Subsidiary]
	Balance internal pressure to invest in firm specific assets and external pressures to meet customer needs. A good balance may allow the parent company to leverage skills that the subsidiary has accumulated, as well as to benefit from economies of scale because of the subsidiary's expanded transaction volume.

Ex-post Lock-in of Group Boundary

After a subsidiary has been established, other make or buy criteria such as utilization exist. High switching cost and biases that justify using subsidiary over market may prolong lock-in, such that high internal transaction costs outweigh external transaction costs.

[Type IND Subsidiary]

Balance between centrifugal and centripetal forces may be sought when the subsidiary is seen as a crucial element in rebuilding the group's synergy.[6] The degree of lock-in differs depending on the type of subsidiary.

[Type 1 Subsidiary]

The parent company could choose to use the market, but needs to consider utilization rate and profitability of the subsidiary.

[Type M Subsidiary]

Because of mutual dependence, lock-in will occur when there are high switching costs. This becomes problematic when locked-in routines are inefficient.

[Type 2 Subsidiary]

The parent dependence on the subsidiary forms a kind of lock-in, and this becomes problematic when there exists conflicting interests between the parent company's and the subsidiary, such as when the subsidiary, in focusing on external businesses, fails to invest in firm-specific skills.

(*Continued*)

---

[6]Such was the case with Panasonic's subsidiary Panasonic Electric Works, which was hived off from Matsushita (former name of Panasonic) in 1935. The company had great autonomy as an IND related company until it became Panasonic's subsidiary in 2004, when Panasonic increased ownership to 51%. Later in 2011, as part of Panasonic's restructuring, Panasonic Electric Works became Panasonic's wholly owned subsidiary. The company's strength in electric works was regarded by Panasonic as a crucial competence in its solutions business, and in January 2012, it was dissolved and absorbed by Panasonic, thus ending the company's 76-year history.

Table 11: (*Continued*)

Academic and Practitioner's Knowledge	Types of Subsidiary
Vertical and Horizontal Coordination: Managers and workers who have proper understanding of central management instructions, adjust those instructions using the local information that they perfectly observe. Benefits of coordination have to outweigh communication costs.	The benefits of investing in the coordination and transfer of knowledge and information have to outweigh the costs of doing so. Very often, this depends on the type of subsidiary. [Type 1 Subsidiary] Little coordination is needed because the parent is not dependent on the subsidiary's output. [Type M Subsidiary]
Decentralization and Delegation of Decision Rights: Select appropriate level of decentralization based on the costs and benefits of delegation. Costs: Incentive cost, control loss and power abuse. Benefits: Access to local information, better and quicker decision-making.	Because of mutual dependence, and especially when the subsidiary is integrated into parent company's production value chain, coordination systems will be used more widely to align incentives and knowledge. [Type 2 Subsidiary] Because of dual pressures internally and externally, conflict may require more careful coordination. Managers who are seconded or transferred from the parent company may act at effective mediators.
Coordination Systems: Corporate groups have multiple coordination systems that are used alongside decentralization and delegation systems.	[Type IND Subsidiary] IND subsidiaries may have more autonomy because there is little dependency relationship. However, delegation may be contingent upon performance of the subsidiary, which the parent company monitors.

Parent–Subsidiary Relationship:

Dual pressures that could lead to conflict. Normative integration through socialization could reduce conflict.

Agency problems may arise such that subsidiaries may pursue interests that diverge from the corporate group's goals. This can be reduced by monitoring and by designing incentive compatible contracts.

Coordination systems facilitate the diffusion of knowledge between the parent company and the subsidiary.

[Type 1 Subsidiary]

Weak bargaining power deems it necessary for the subsidiary to give in to demands made by the parent company.

[Type M Subsidiary]

Mutual dependence deems it necessary for the parent company and the subsidiary to coordinate regularly, and decision making may be more centralized.

[Type 2 Subsidiary]

Agency problems may arise when external pressures are in conflict with internal pressures.

[Type IND Subsidiary]

The subsidiary has more autonomy because there is little interdependency; but may be contingent upon its performance and contribution to the group.

A major implication of differences in subsidiary types is that control and coordination need to take these into consideration in order to be effective. From discussions with corporate managers, many corporations do not seem to be aware or conscious of these differences, and it is, therefore, possible that the mutually agreed outcomes of their coordination processes may not be optimal. Using the typology matrix though, many companies in my discussion group were able to identify their current parent–subsidiary relationship, and adjust to better ways of coordinating activities. For example, in one company, the counter-part head-office department, in addition to applying standardized financial monitoring on its Type M subsidiary, started benchmarking price and performance with other companies in the same industry.

Chapter 8

ROADMAP TO CREATING A SUCCESSFUL SUBSIDIARY

Having reviewed the major literatures and case study materials in the previous chapters, I devote this chapter to discussing how a corporate group could create a successful subsidiary by following four simple steps. Although it would be impossible to prescribe a success formula for all corporations and their subsidiaries, and any such attempt would be far too ambitious, I hope to use the roadmap analogy to highlight what companies should consider, when thinking about managing subsidiaries.

8.1 STEP-1. CONSIDER FIRST YOUR OPTIONS AND THEIR LIFESPAN

Much academic knowledge has focused on the *make or buy* decision making based on the transaction cost theory. For example, when there is uncertainty and when it is hard to observe external suppliers such that undesirable *ex-post* opportunistic behaviour should be avoided, then having the function in-house may be a better option especially when, according to property rights theory, there are high complementarities between assets and capabilities that favours ownership. Depending on what the company needs to balance, such as internal and external transaction costs, it may choose amongst available options, ranging from the market to in-house division, including the intermediate organization which we call the subsidiary.

If it is a new *make or buy* decision, considerations need also to be given to the possibility of *ex-post* lock-in, for once established, a subsidiary has to be utilised efficiently. The lifespan of that option needs to be considered too, because what may appear now to a highly firm-specific product that justifies in-house production by a subsidiary, may in just a few years' time turn out to be so modularized that it would become cheaper and more efficient to procure the product from the market. For example, one of the case study companies has a Type M maintenance subsidiary which operates in a restricted customs zone area, and hence enjoys a high barrier to entry. But recently it became possible and feasible for other companies to operate outside the restricted area, such that the parent company now has the option to use those companies that are cheaper than using its subsidiary. The subsidiary too suddenly finds itself exposed to outside competition, and in terms of parent–subsidiary relationship, it has shifted from Type M to Type 1, with rather grim prospects of winning business from the parent company. The parent may decide to continue its trading with that subsidiary, or it may decide that the life-span of the subsidiary has come to an end.

Although not all future events can be anticipated *ex-ante*, the possibility of an interrupted lifespan needs to be considered too, especially when there is a high probability of disruptive technologies that could affect the company's production value chain.

(a) Careful consideration is needed prior to establishing a subsidiary, especially on the anticipated life-span of the subsidiary. Comparisons with other strategic options should be made based on the assumed life-span.

(b) Effectiveness and role of the subsidiary needs to be periodically evaluated. Internal and external environment may change to affect the life-span of the subsidiary differently from what was initially planned.

(c) Life-span can be assigned to a subsidiary. Often referred to as a "Captive Unit", a subsidiary can be established with the purpose of serving a function over a period of time during which it is a source of required key competence, but also with the purpose of subsequent IPO and capital gain when it is no longer a source of competence to the corporation. Capital gain from the captive unit can then be used as a means to secure resource needed for investing in the next required competence.

8.2 STEP-2. IDENTIFY THE CURRENT PARENT AND SUBSIDIARY RELATIONSHIP

Many firms that I have talked to said they do not have a satisfactory way of classifying subsidiaries that could help term evaluate their subsidiaries' roles and performances. Using the typology matrix described in Chapter 7 could help stakeholders have a clear understanding first about the existing state of parent–subsidiary dependency relationship and whether it is consistent with the company's strategy, before proceeding further to address management problems such as alignment with corporate strategy. The typology matrix allows both the parent and the subsidiary to discuss issues from their own perspectives as well as their counterpart's perspective. This dual perspective helps facilitate discussion, and can be used to produce mutual agreed solution, which is an important characteristic of the parent–subsidiary relationship in Japanese corporations because it allows control and coordination to function alongside decentralization. Table 12 gives an example of how the tool can be used.

The important takeaway here is that the role of a subsidiary as perceived by the parent company may not be a complete one, and it is only when we add the perspective of the subsidiary that the picture becomes more complete. A more complete and shared understanding helps the parent company and subsidiary to coordinate better and make better judgements.

Table 12: Examples of problem solving by subsidiary type

Subsidiary Type and Direction of Dependence	Subsidiary's Position	Parent Company's Position
Type 1 Parent → Subsidiary	The parent company is the only client, such that when the parent company cuts production or procurement, the subsidiary loses its sole source of revenue. The subsidiary tries to find other external clients but has not been successful.	It is cheaper to procure from the market because the product has become much modularized and commoditized. But doing so will reduce operation rate of its subsidiary as well as incur losses, which the parent company has to cover.
	Mutually Agreed Solution: Parent company to transfer skills to the subsidiary to help improve productivity. Subsidiary to strive to be as competitive as the market. If improvements are not made within the agreed timeframe, the parent company will close down subsidiary or change to use its resources for production in another business division.	
Type 2 Parent → Subsidiary	As a business subsidiary, it is generating profits, but it faces constant pressure from the parent company parent to focus its production resources on the parent company's product, as well as to cut down on investments that are considered not firm specific to the parent.	Depends heavily on inputs from the subsidiary and hence exerts centripetal pressure. However, the parent has also benefited much from the economies of scale its subsidiary has attained through business with external clients.
	Mutually Agreed Solution: Decided that the subsidiary should give priority to the parent company's product, which is a required competence in the corporate group's core growth driver business.	

Type M Parent ⇔ Subsidiary	Business with the parent company has become routine and there is no need to worry about fierce competition (which having external businesses would entail). Although there is no intentional milking of profits from the parent company, there is little incentive to innovate.	The subsidiary provides highly firm specific products that cannot be procured from the market. Hence it is not easy to determine transaction price for there is no market price to allow comparison. The business unit is profitable so there is little incentive to stretch its subsidiary's targets.
	Mutually Agreed Solution: Decided to use non-financial KPIs to monitor and stretch performance, and also to monitor subsidiary's procurement costs	
Type IND Parent (independent) Subsidiary	Profitable business subsidiary with relative high degree of autonomy.	Noticed that multiple business subsidiaries are developing and producing similar products.
	Mutually Agreed Solution: Decided to combine multiple businesses and rebrand the corporate group as a fully integrated solutions provider.	

8.3 STEP-3. ALIGN YOUR PARENT–SUBSIDIARY RELATIONSHIP TO STRATEGY

Having identified the subsidiary type based on existing parent–subsidiary relationship, the next step is to define or re-define the role of the subsidiary to make sure that it is aligned to the corporate strategy. A mutually agreed solution between the parent company and the subsidiary may result in the role of the subsidiary remaining unchanged, or it may result in the subsidiary shifting from one subsidiary type to another.

We saw in the case of Hitachi that, subsidiaries are encouraged to be entrepreneurial and that the delegation of decision rights is contingent upon the subsidiary's performance, such that the subsidiary, in knowing that the better it performs, the more bargaining power and discretion it will have in operating its businesses, will have the incentives to invest in further efforts. Clarity in roles and responsibilities enables subsidiary to be independent value generators.

One important activity in this process of role definition lies in recognizing the capabilities of the subsidiary. As Birkinshaw (1995) has pointed out, parent companies are not always aware of their subsidiaries' capabilities, and a subsidiary's contributory role within the corporate group depends greatly on the parent and subsidiary relationship, the subsidiary's initiative and entrepreneurism, and the parent company's recognition of the subsidiary's capabilities. A subsidiary's role is not static and often changes along with the business environment and with expectations from the parent company. I will use the examples of Shiseido and Hitachi to illustrate how their subsidiary roles have changed over time.

Example 1: Shiseido's shift from in-house logistics to outsourced logistics.

The cosmetics company Shisedo had a 100% owned logistics functional subsidiary, which specialized in delivering millions of product items from factories to distribution centres, from distribution centres to its national network of product centres, and from thence to various types of retailers such as chain stores, convenience stores, drug stores, department stores, home centres, and retail agents. Due to various changes in business environment, Shiseido's market share plummeted, and costs kept on rising as customer demand became more fragmented and complicated. Its logistics subsidiary found itself to be no longer capable of handling all of Shiseido's logistics requirements effectively.

In response to these and other pressing issues, Shiseido's headquarter decided to focus all its investments on its core businesses. The logistics subsidiary, which was regarded as a non-core business, was sold to a major 3PL company, Hitachi Transport Systems. In shifting from in-house logistics to outsourcing, Shiseido was able to be more responsive to logistics needs, to reduce logistics costs, to avoid investments in costly logistics facilities, and to turn logistics costs from fixed costs into variable costs. As this example shows, the mutually agreed solution was for the company to outsource its logistics rather than to invest in building competencies of its logistics subsidiary.

Example 2: From functional subsidiary to a successful business subsidiary.

Hitachi Transport Systems, which took over Shiseido's logistics subsidiary, began as a functional subsidiary that specialized in providing logistic services to Hitachi Group. It developed capabilities through its business within Hitachi, leverage those capabilities, and expanded its business by providing logistics to other companies. Hitachi Transport Systems grew from a functional subsidiary to being a listed business subsidiary and a major logistics service provider in Japan, ranking top amongst 3PL companies by sales revenue.

Note that in Example 2, Hitachi Transport Systems has dual roles of being both a profit centre as well as a cost centre. The strategy is not either to be a cost centre or a profit centre, but both cost and profit centres. And there are several good reasons to believe why this AND strategy works. A functional subsidiary has to be an excellent in-house service or product provider first before it could compete in the market against other competitors, and deliver offerings to other companies who may have their own specialized functional subsidiary. In fact, the subsidiary has to be excellent to the point that even external clients would prefer using it to using their own specialized functional subsidiaries. In other words, the subsidiary must have some proprietary advantage to compensate for the natural disadvantage of competing with established firms in a different industry. This is no easy hurdle to clear and the bar is indeed very high. But as the example of Hitachi shows, it is possible. By shifting from Type M to Type 2, a functional subsidiary can increase knowledge of its business, and may also benefit from economies of scale that would enable it to succeed both as a cost centre and a profit centre. However, moving from Type M to Type 2 may create parent–subsidiary conflict when interests collide, which is why agreeing on the role and responsibility of the subsidiary is important.

Another hurdle is that the parent company may not be aware of the subsidiary's full potential, and without the parent company's consent or delegation of decision rights, the subsidiary would not be able to invest in expanding its business from Type M to Type 2. Coordination and control by the parent company can, therefore, either promote or inhibit the subsidiary's contributor role. The important activity of this step, therefore, is to work out a mutually acceptable solution based on well informed knowledge concerning the subsidiary's capabilities and the corporate group's overall optimality.

8.4 STEP-4. TAILOR CONTROL AND COORDINATION SYSTEMS, AND MONITOR CHANGES

After having identified the subsidiary type and having mutually agreed on the role and commitment of the subsidiary, the next step would be to tailor control and coordination systems that best fits the parent–subsidiary setting as shown in Table 13.

Because firms need to respond and adapt to changes in business environments, the actions described in the above steps need to be reviewed and revised accordingly. Appropriate monitoring is needed to ensure that control and coordination systems are effective. It is also important to understand and make trade-offs decisions. Table 14 provides some examples of trade-offs that may have to be considered.

Table 13: Example of different focus of control and coordination based on subsidiary type

	Coordination	Delegation	Relationship
Type 1	Improve competitiveness, for example, by coaching and transferring skills from parent company.	Foster independent-ness and entrepreneurship.	Quasi-market like relationship, though need also to consider utilization and revenue of subsidiary.
Type M	Work closely to share tacit knowledge and to leverage capabilities of subsidiaries.	Because of dependency, major decisions may be centralised. Need clear role definition to empower and maintain incentives.	Be careful not to let routine transactions breed inefficiencies. Benchmark market prices, and where necessary, revise trading terms.
Type 2	Control subsidiary as both profit and cost centre. Decide whether scarce resources should be used to develop firm specific competencies for the company or for external businesses.	Increase control when there appears to be conflicting interests that could negatively affect the overall optimality of the corporate group.	Conflict of interest may arise because of dual pressures from internal and external businesses. Try to mutually agree on scenario that maximizes group performance.
Type IND	Coordination centred on portfolio management and on overall optimality. Part of the subsidiary may be severed from the subsidiary's control and incorporated instead into the group's growth driver division.	Delegation contingent upon performance. Despite autonomy that is granted to the subsidiary, if it constitutes a major source of revenue to the group, then decision rights on major strategic issues may still rest on the parent company.	Relationship likely to be closer if the subsidiary is a core business or if it has synergies with the group's core business, and distant if it is a non-core business.

Table 14:   Trade-offs that may need to be considered during coordination

	Examples of Trade-offs	
Step-1 Consider options and their lifespan	Monitoring and evaluation may reveal the fact that it is better to procure from the market rather than from one's subsidiary because trading terms are more propitious.	If the subsidiary is a Type 1, using the market may cause the subsidiary and consequently the corporate group to suffer losses.
Step-2 Identify subsidiary type	May agree to have subsidiary focus on internal transaction within the group. But the absence of market discipline may gradually lead to inefficiencies. The subsidiary may also lack outside exposure and opportunity to upgrade their competences, or to benefit from economies of scale by having more clients.	May agree to shift from Type M to Type 2 or Type IND, but this would be highly risky if the subsidiary does not have any proprietary advantage over established firms.
Step-3 Mutually agree and define the role of the subsidiary		
Step-4 Tailor control and coordination that best fit the subsidiary type. Have appropriate level of monitoring and control over the subsidiary.	Delegation can speed up decision-making, and can allow the company to utilize local information that is not accessible by the parent. Rotations, secondments and transfers are effective in bridging cognitions between the parent company and the subsidiary. Coordination allows the parent company to transfer specialized skills to the subsidiary. Monitoring reduces agency problems, and should be used to complement delegation of power to subsidiaries.	In addition to control loss and agency problems, decentralization and delegation can lead to uncoordinated activities and wasteful duplication of efforts in unchecked. Rotations may create high overhead costs. Secondments and transfers may hurt incentives of the subsidiary's employees when they occupy most of the senior positions and hinder advancement. Excessive monitoring may hurt the subsidiary's incentives to invest in efforts.

Chapter 9

CONCLUSION AND AREAS FOR FUTURE RESEARCH

In this work, I have examined the research questions concerning why corporations form groups and how corporations manage their vast number of subsidiaries. These questions are relevant and important because the number of Japanese firms using subsidiaries are increasing. Also, subsidiaries essentially make up a substantial part of a corporate group's activities and competencies. The effectiveness of management systems that Japanese firms use in managing their subsidiaries can, therefore, have substantial impact on performance and on the Japanese economy as well.

In Chapter 4, I looked at the main theories and academic literatures that address the question of why firms create subsidiaries and form groups. One economic rationale, from both transaction cost perspective as well as a property rights perspectives, is that subsidiaries are used as a means to balance high external transaction costs of using the market and high internal transaction costs that arise from control that reduces productivity. It also balances control when there are high costs to allocating ownership control rights exclusively to the parent. The rationale here is based on the premise that control may reduce productivity. This argument is consistent with incentive theories that posit that subsidiary is a means to solve incentive problems, where agents who foresee

149

ex-ante that management will renege on its promise and intervene *ex-post*, will hold back incentives to invest in efforts. Commitment by using subsidiaries is, therefore, seen as an effective solution. This incentive rationale appears to be supported by empirical research which showed that incentive is one of the main reasons for firms hiving-off subsidiaries.

With regards to the case studies, my main findings and their implications are as follows:

1. Coordination and mutual agreement enables delegation to be used alongside control

In the case studies I observed in many occasions where the delegation of decision rights to subsidiaries is used alongside control by the parent company. Such practice, according to incentive theory, would appear to defeat the purpose of forming subsidiaries, which is to enhance incentives by restricting *ex-post* intervention. The case studies show that this does not have to be the case. Firstly, the amount of power delegation to subsidiaries often depends on the activity that is concerned. There is usually more control over strategic issues that could affect the parent company, but less control and more delegation over operational issues. Secondly, as I have learnt from the case studies, firms usually have control and coordination systems such as subsidiary counter-part head-office departments that coordinate activities with subsidiaries without destroying incentives. They actually enhance incentives as coordination eliminates uncertainties in human exchange, and so instead of being restrictive, they enable subsidiaries to act freely as long as they do not violate agreements that have been made with the parent company. The case studies also revealed an emphasis on mutual agreement in coordination processes between the parent and the subsidiary. Hitachi's case, in which subsidiaries commit to certain performance levels, and the parent company grants the subsidiaries autonomy contingent upon whether their promises and commitments have been kept, is a good example that shows how mutually agreed rules help players play more effectively.

2. The extent to which the transaction cost balance rationale holds depends on the subsidiary type

Although it was not so obvious when I first started this research, the more I talked to companies, the more I became acutely aware that there are many different types of subsidiaries, and this insight opened up new avenues to my research on subsidiaries, because for each of the theories that I have discussed in this book, such as the delegation of decision rights, control and coordination, parent and subsidiary relationship, dual pressures and conflict, whether they concur with practice depends on the type of subsidiary at question.

In order to conduct an in-depth analysis on subsidiaries, I constructed a four-part classification of subsidiaries based on the interdependency relationship between the parent and the subsidiary.

There are several reasons for using dependency as a criterion. When I started conducting interviews for the case studies, I often found it confusing as to whether the role of the subsidiary that was described to me was the role as seen from the parent company's perspective or from the subsidiary's perspective. For example, the parent may regard the subsidiary as one of many suppliers in the market, while the subsidiary may regard the parent as its sole client. Or the parent company may depend on the subsidiary for inputs, while the subsidiary may depend not on the parent company but on external clients as its major source of revenue. Viewing the role of a subsidiary from both parent company and subsidiary perspectives helps present a more complete picture of their relationship. This is useful, because different relationships produce different coordination issues that require different ways of managing them.

Despite the expectation derived from theory that the use of subsidiary balances internal and external transaction costs, I found, by looking into each subsidiary type, that this is not always the case. In the case of Type 1 subsidiary, it appears that neither high internal cost nor high external cost demands much concern because the parent company is not dependent on the subsidiary, and very often uses external suppliers. Likewise, the concern for balance of costs for Type IND is also expected to be small because there is little dependency on the subsidiary.

In the case of Type M and Type 2 subsidiaries, since the parent company is dependent on them for their outputs, the concern for balance of internal and external costs may be more relevant as the parent company may fear that excessive control would curb incentives and reduce productivity. But even here, it is dubious as to whether it is the cost balance that matters. For Type M, very often a relatively high level of control is unavoidable, and hence the issue here is perhaps less about reducing control and more about devising mechanisms such as mutual consent and socialization that would sustain incentives. As for Type 2 subsidiaries, because of the tension and conflicting interests that could arise from internal and external pressures, control may be contingent upon the amount of tension that exists.

Being a subsidiary alone does not necessarily guarantee a balanced level of control, and as illustrated above, there are cases where it is deemed necessary for the parent company to exert hierarchical like control over its subsidiaries. It is also the case that control does not necessarily damage incentives. The MHI case shows for example that control and coordination systems are used also as a means to align incentives, mediate differences, and mitigate damages to incentives.

3. Subsidiary type may change over time, deeming it necessary to review rationale

Using subsidiaries provide the firm with a wider range of options to choose from, and hence more flexibility to cope with contingencies. Because subsidiaries are essentially intermediate organizations, the parent company can choose to use hierarchical control or market like transaction towards its subsidiary, contingent upon the situation at hand. One important implication here is that such contingencies mean at the same time that the role of subsidiaries can vary and change, and the degree of ownership and control too can vary and change.

A subsidiary may shift from Type M to Type 1 so as to enhance competitiveness, or a parent company may rewrite its relationship with its subsidiary from Type M to Type 1 when it needs to acquire new knowledge that is not accessible inside the corporate. Even in the case of Type IND, a parent company may, in the process of rebuilding its group's synergy, delist its Type IND subsidiary from the stock exchange, and place it under its own business division. For example, in 2011, we witnessed Panasonic's full ownership of Panasonic Electric Works, and in 2012, Hitachi Solutions' full ownership of Hitachi Business Solution, and Hitachi Metals' full ownership of Hitachi Tool.

The implication of such shifts is that the original rationale when the subsidiary was formed could change over time, such that it may no longer be aligned to the current corporate strategy. In one group study session, a head office manager said to me that the use of the typology matrix shown in Figure 17 has helped his company and its subsidiary to identify where they currently stand, and which direction they should head forward to.

4. Different subsidiary type have different focuses and hence require different balance and coordination

The case studies also revealed that the companies have different ways of coordinating activities, delegating decision rights, and balancing trade-offs, depending on the type of subsidiary. For example, while the parent company of a Type M subsidiary may be concerned about removing inefficiencies that may have crept in from mutual dependency, the parent company of a Type 2 subsidiary may be concerned about whether to allocate scarce corporate resources for more internal production and less external businesses or vice versa. The focuses are different and, therefore, the control and coordination mechanisms that work best may be different too.

Understanding the different ways in which parent companies and subsidiaries interact and evaluating whether the current relationship fits the corporation's strategy may yield insights that could help a corporation re-engineer its activities and re-define its corporate boundaries. However, it appears that many companies do not always have a clear picture as to why they have subsidiaries, and together with corporate inertia, this may seriously hinder strategy execution. This study, therefore, provides a practical tool which practitioners could use to map out parent and subsidiary relationships and tailor manage and coordinate processes better. It can also be used to analyze how theory would work differently under different subsidiary types.

There are, however, many limitations in this work. Although the research material was gathered from 14 corporate groups, the level of detail is still insufficient, and a more thorough empirical research would be needed to establish a reliable link between the proposed typology and academic theories on corporate groups. Although I have discussed in this book that the cost balance rationale does not hold for all four types of subsidiaries, I have not fully answered the question of what alternative rationale then best explains each of the four types of subsidiary. Further empirical research would be required to investigate how control and coordination work within each different type of subsidiaries, so as to identify whether the coordination systems that are employed are effective. These gaps could be a possible topic for further research.

APPENDIX: REASONS FOR ESTABLISHING SUBSIDIARIES

Parent Company	Subsidiary	To Develop Business	To Strengthen Function or Capability
1 Avex Group Holdings	Avex Shanghai	Growing live entertainment market in China	
2 Azuma Shipping	Donghua Cargo Agency		Expand and improve logistics services
3 Onkyo	Joint venture subsidiary		Combine synergies of Onkyo's audio systems with Gibson's music instruments
4 CyberAgent	Sirok		Application development for smart phone
5 House Food	House Foods Vietnam	Overseas markets as drivers of growth	
6 Nidec	Nidec Management Shanghai		Strengthen financial management
7 Toray	Toray Carbon Fibers Europe	Global growth in demand for carbon material	Strengthen production vertical integration
8 Fujitsu	New subsidiary		Consolidate software development subsidiaries
9 Mitsubishi Gas Chemical	Manufacturing plant in Thailand		Mitigate supply chain risk in response to 3.11 magnitude earthquake
10 Proto	Car Credo	Growing demand for inspection certification of used cars	Integrate to include car inspection function
11 Mcea	Good-Timing	IT Ventures	
12 Furukawa Electric	Furukawa Automotive Systems Lima Philippines		Wire harness manufacturing and sales

13 Commerce21	100% subsidiary	Growth potential of e-commerce business in Singapore and S.E. Asia	Strengthen publishing management
14 Klab	Klab International (Singapore)	Market expansion of social media via smart phone	Strengthen production capability
15 Nissin Kogyo	Alcar Chemo Indonesia	Market potential in Asia for automotive products	Copper bonding wire manufacturing
16 Tanaka Holdings	Subsidiary in Taiwan		Development of social games via smart phone
17 DeNA	DeNA Studios Canada		
18 Macromill	Embrain	Global expansion to underdeveloped market in Korea and Asia	Combine synergies of Macromill's panel data with Embrain's marketing research
19 Kitagawa Iron Works	Kitagawa Mexico	Growing demand for automotive products	Manufacturing function near the market
20 Fan Communications	Ad Japan	Growing need for Japanese advertising agency abroad	Plan and provide multilingual services
21 Gree	Subsidiary in Osaka	Expand business to market in India	Application software development
22 Ricoh	Ricoh Innovations Private Ltd		
23 Globalknowledge	Globalknowledge Management Center	Growing demand for training global professionals	
24 News2u	100% subsidiary in the U.S.	Expand to become provider of global social media	Marketing and sales of News2u's global services

(Continued)

Appendix   (*Continued*)

Parent Company	Subsidiary	To Develop Business	To Strengthen Function or Capability
25 Voyage Group	Socialand	To enter into business of marketing support for social media	
26 Nippon Konpo	Nippon Konpo Hochiminh	Expand logistic business to South Vietnam	
27 Adways	Adways Philippines	Large market demand in Asian countries for social media marketing tools	Develop and release marketing tools for corporate clients
28 DRB-Hicom	DRB-Hicom Leasing(Malaysia)	Expand auto lease business	
29 Mitsubishi Corporation	Subsidiary in Canada	Expand natural gas development business	Joint Venture to acquire drilling rights for natural gas
30 Chubu Electric Power	Chubu Energy Trading Singapore		Strengthen coal procurement function (Singapore being trading centre in Asia)
31 Ajinomoto	NRI System Techno		Merge existing IT subsidiary with NRI to acquire capabilities
32 Alsok	Alsok Malaysia	Respond to demands from Japanese firms in Malaysia for security services	
33 I-O Data	ITG Marketing		Handle import and sales of solid state drive products
34 Aiming	Aiming Korea	Expand online and mobile dame business to Korea	Market in Korea software application developed by Aiming

35	Hitachi	Hitachi Plant Qatar	Growing demand for infrastructure business	Joint venture for engineering, procurement, and construction
36	CDG	CDG Promotional Marketing(USA)	Leverage skills developed in Japan to expand marketing business overseas	
37	Transcosmos	Transcosmos China	Expand call centre business in China to capture increasing demand	
38	Asahi Kasei	Subsidiary in the U.S.	Acquire ZOLL Medical to enter growth market in emergency medical service	
39	Iwatani	Iwatani-SIG Industrial Gases		Joint venture in Singapore to supply liquid fuel and gases to local factories
40	NTT Docomo	Two new subsidiaries	Seek new revenue source by diversifying to new businesses through partnerships	Create synergies by joining complementary assets. (logistics + smart phone)
41	Laox	Subsidiary in China	Expand home appliance retail network in China	
42	King Jim	Subsidiary in Hong Kong	Foothold for expansion in the growing Asian market	

(Continued)

Appendix   *(Continued)*

Parent Company	Subsidiary	To Develop Business	To Strengthen Function or Capability
43 Hoya	Hoya Visual Company	Enhance presence in S. America and capture its large growing market	
44 Orion	Orion Machinery Asia	Dual purpose of overseas manufacturing and overseas market expansion	Manufacture air dryer and vacuum pump products for Asian market
45 Denso	3D		To improve visual image display capability in automotive products
46 Teijin	R&D subsidiary	Pioneer CFRP market	Develop carbon fiber reinforced plastics material for automobile frame
47 Hitachi	Hitachi Air Conditioning Europe		Combine regional airconditioning sales function to manufacturing function
48 Sumitomo Corporation	Subsidiary in the U.S.		Joint development of wind farm
49 Showa	Showa Autoparts (Vietnam)	Expand production and sales to capture growing demand for motorcycle	Manufacture of automotive parts
50 Fujitsu	Fujitsu Mobile Communications		Acquire remaining shares from Toshiba to strengthen mobile phone business
51 Kyocera	Kyocera CTC (India)	Capture demand for industrial machinery equipment	Manufacture and sales of industrial machinery equipment

52	Japan Cablenet (JCN)	Acquired subsidiary	Acquisition of cable TV station as part of growth strategy	
53	Cybernet Systems	Subsidiary in Korea		Sales subsidiary to market its MapleSim products in Korea
54	Cybernet Systems	Noesis Solutions LLC (U.S.)		Sales subsidiary to market Noesis products in the U.S.
55	Toyobo	Toyobo Industrial Materials America	Capture demand for air-bag material	Sales subsidiary to strengthen air-bag business in the U.S.
56	Toyota	Subsidiary in China	Develop green environment business in China	Develop synergies with Suntory Midorie
57	Klab Global	Klab America		Market social media games in the U.S.
58	NTT Data	Subsidiary in Myanmar	Capture business growth potentials in Myanmar	
59	Panasonic	Panasonic Eco Solutions North America	Develop eco solution business in the U.S.	
60	Mitsui Corporation	Mitsui Global Investment India	Investment opportunities in India	Strengthen private equity function
61	Paperboy&co	Hived-off subsidiaries		Hived-off two business units to speed up decision making
62	Transcosmos	Transcosmos Analytics	Develop CRM research and consulting business	
63	Gree	Acquired subsidiary		Synergies by combining Gree platform with Funzio's high quality game

(Continued)

Appendix   (*Continued*)

Parent Company	Subsidiary	To Develop Business	To Strengthen Function or Capability
64 Nippon Konpo	Nippon Konpo Vietnam Real Estate		Leasing of logistic facilities
65 Dwango	Qteras		Strengthen service development of its consumer electronics division
66 Soft Bank Technology	Subsidiary in Korea	Expand EC-BPO business in Asia	
67 Soft Bank	Paypal Japan		Establish default standard of in-line payment via smart phone
68 Proto	Subsidiary in Singapore		Strengthen used car information business in Asia
69 Fast Retailing	Subsidiary in China		Speed up expansion of Uniqlo retail stores in China
70 GK Line	GK Communications	To capture market growth in the Philippines	
71 Showa Denko	Shanghai Showa Electronic Chemical Materials		Strengthen manufacturing and sales of high-purity gases handling equipment
72 JTB	JTB Research		Strengthen research and marketing of tourism
73 NTT Communications	NTT Com Marketing		Consolidate resources to strengthen sales and marketing
74 Ricoh	Ricoh Thermal Media Asia	Capture demand in emerging markets in the Asia-Pacific region	Build customer-centric manufacturing and sales functions in India

75 Taisho Phamaceutical	Acquisition of Tokuhon		Strengthen line-up of over the counter medical products
76 Noritake	100% ownership of KCM Corporation		Strengthen R&D capability, and develop fuel battery market
77 Sansei Yusoki	Acquisition of Telmic		Strengthen synergies
78 Starzen	100% ownership of Lohmeyer		Strengthen and centralize strategic function, speed up decision making
79 NTT Data	NTT Data Financial Solutions		Acquire TGIFS's skills in financial market
80 Uemura	PT Uemura Indonesia		Strengthen technical support system to expand sales
81 Sonet Entertainment	Samepot Korea	Capture growth in on-line game industry	Strengthen game development capabilities
82 Cygames	CyDesignation		Strengthen development of game application
83 Inui Steamship	Inui Shipping Singapore		Strengthen handy bulker business
84 NEC	NEC Korea		Strengthen local capability to support solution provider business
85 Komehyo	Komehyo Auction		Plan, operate and manage auction of used items
86 Sega	Sega Networks	Expand and maximize revenue from its network business	Globalize contents of its smart phone and tablet. Speed up decision making
87 Fujikoshi	Nachi KG Technology India	Develop bearing business in India	Manufacture and sales of automobile bearings

(Continued)

Appendix   (*Continued*)

Parent Company	Subsidiary	To Develop Business	To Strengthen Function or Capability
88 D2C	Kakezan		Strengthen creative capabilities and solution business
89 Gree	Gree Canada		Strengthen operation and development of social games
90 Classico	Subsidiary in U.S. and Taiwan		Strengthen product development based on local customer needs
91			
92 Toyota Enterprise	Toyota Enterprise India	Develop interior facility and service business in India	
93 Kyoshin	Kyoshin Language Academy	Expand Japanese language school business	
94 Tokai Rubber Industries	Tokai Rubber Chemical and Plastic Products		Production and sales of OA machine parts in Thailand
95 Sony	100% ownership of So-net	Acquire So-net's high potential investments	
96 Vector	Initial		To increase variety of services in response to customer needs
97 Members	Engagement First	Capture corporate demand for engagement marketing	Strengthen consulting business in engagement marketing using social media
98 Rakuten	Rakuten Emobile		To provide high-speed LTE service and expand service network
99 Snowpeak	Snowpeak Well		To enhance CSR and contribute to community

100 Siam Cosmos Services	Cosmos Services	Capture growing business opportunities in Vietnam	Sell insurance services to consumers in Vietnam
101 Aeon	Aeon Bike	Expand lifecycle concept as part of restructuring of supermarket business	Hived-off from BU to specialize in bicycle retail business
102 Tokai Rubber Industries	Tokai Rubber Hose Vietnam	Capture growing demand for motocycles	Manufacture rubber tires for motocycles
103 Klab Global	Klab China		Develop localized marketing and products for Japanese market. Reduce costs
104 Mitsubishi Corporation	Joint venture subsidiary	Long-term contract to supply energy to Jordan	Power plant as part of IPP (Independent Power Producer) project
105 Avex Group Holdings	Uula		Distribute AV contents to smart phone users
106 Hitachi Plant Technology	New joint venture subsidiary		Combine competencies to create synergy in infrastructure solution business
107 Gala	Gala Innovative		Development of social game
108 Socialwire	Cross Coop Philippines	Capture demand of Japanese firms setting up overseas operations	Office lease business targeted towards Japanese clients
109 Kimura Information Technology	KIT International	Respond to customer demand for broadcast from abroad	Broadcast medical news to Japan
110 Logitem	Subsidiary in Vietnam		Strengthen import/export and sales function
111 Kyocera Communications	Acquisition of MOTEX		Need competence in information security software

(*Continued*)

Appendix *(Continued)*

Parent Company	Subsidiary	To Develop Business	To Strengthen Function or Capability
112 Freebit	Subsidiary in Hong Kong		Provide cloud service to clients in China
113 Hino Motors	Hino Motors Manufacturing Malaysia		Secure supply to meet growing demand from sales
114 Yoshinoya Holdings	Joint venture subsidiary		Complementarity with partner's strong business network in China
115 Carview	Carview Kenya	Capture growing demand for imported used cars from Japan	
116 Irep	Subsidiary in Japan		Provide digital marketing services to medium-small size firms
117 Fujitsu	IT Management Partners		Combine outsourcing service centres to reduce cost
118 Hokto	Hokto Malaysia	Expand business in S.E. Asia	Growing and sales of mushrooms
119 Rakuten	Acquisition o Alpha Direct Service		Strengthen logistics function to support growing EC business
120 Adways	Adways Korea	Capture high growth in Korea of smartphone business	Provide advertisement services using smart phone
121 Koito	Subsidiary in Mexico	Capture growing automobile demand in Mexico	Manufacture automobile lightings
122 Sato Group	Sato Vietnam Solutions		Provide solutions using auto-recognition systems

123 CyberAgent	CyberSS	Capture growing demand in advertisements using smart phone	Provide tools for smart phone advertisements
124 HIS	Subsidiary in Thailand	Establish airline that specializes in charter flight	
125 Excite	Excite Media Services Philippines		Strengthen value offering and business capabilities
126 Topy Industries	Joint venture subsidiary in Indonesia		Manufacture wheels for bus and truck
127 SoftBank Technology	Subsidiary in Korea	Expand EC-BPO Services in S.E. Asia	

Source: News releases from January 2012 to December 2012.

REFERENCES

Abe, T and T Kawakami (2010). Various aspects of situation of institutional economics (*Japanese*). *Shogaku Ronshu*, Vol. 78, No. 4, 23–27.

Aoki, H and H Miyajima (2010). Governance of Business Organizations in Japan — From the Perspective of Firm Boundary and Dual Agency Problem. RIETI Discussion Paper Series 10-J-057 (*Japanese*).

Aoki, H and H Miyajima (2011). Diversification, globalization, corporate group expansion and the governance of business Organizations, Ch. 6. In *Corporate Governance in Japan*, (*Japanese*), H Miyajima, (ed.) RIETI.

Aoki, M (2001). What are institutions? How should we approach them?, Ch. 1. In *Toward a Comparative Institutional Analysis*, MIT Press.

Aoki, M and M Okuno (1996). Comparative institutional analysis of economic systems (*Japanese*), University of Tokyo Press.

Aoki, M (2010). Corporations in Evolving Diversity: Cognition, Governance, and Institutions. Oxford University Press.

Asao, Y (2004). The Government's Role in Human Capital Investment, Accounting Audit, Study No. 30 (*Japanese*).

Bernheim, BD and M Whinston (1990). Multimarket contact and collusive behaviour. *Rand Journal of Economics*, 21(1), 1–26.

Birkinshaw, JM and AJ Morrison (1995). Configurations of strategy and structure in subsidiaries of multinational corporations. *Journal of International Business Studies*, 4, 729–753.

Birkinshaw, J, N Hood and S Jonsson (1998). Building firm-specific advantages in multinational corporations: The role of subsidiary initiative. *Strategic Management Journal*, 19, 221–241.

Birkinshaw, J, N Hood and S Young (2005). Subsidiary entrepreneurship, internal and external competitive forces, and subsidiary performance. *International Business Review,* 14, 227–248.

Blazejewski, S and F Becker-Ritterspach (2011). Conflict in headquarters-subsidiary relations: A critical literature review, Ch. 5. In *Politics and Power in the Multinational Corporation.* Dörrenbächer, C and M Geppert (eds.). Cambridge University Press.

Busemeyer, MR (2009). Asset specificity, institutional complementarities and the variety of skill regimes in coordinated market economies. *Socio Economic Review,* 17(3), 375–406.

Business Research Institute (2011). Management of functional subsidiary, 37th term of the corporate group management study group, Sub-Group 3 Report, Business Research, 3–4 (*Japanese*).

Cabinet Office (2012). Concerning Innovation, Advisory Council on Economic Social Structure (*Japanese*). Minutes of 7th Meeting.

Carney, M, ER Gedajlovic, P Heugens, M van Essan and J van Oosterhout (2011). Business Group Affiliation, Performance, Context, and Strategy: A Meta-Analysis. *Academy of Management Journal,* 15(3), 437–460.

Claessens, S and JPH Fan, LHP Lang (2002). The Benefits and Costs of Group Affiliation. Centre for Economic Policy Research.

Coase, RH (1937). The Nature of the Firms. On-line edition, Wiley online Library, http//onlinelibrary-wiley.com/doi/10.111/j1468.

Deakin, S and HD Whittaker (2009). On a different path? The managerial reshaping of Japanese corporate governance, Ch. 1. In *Corporate Governance and Managerial Reform in Japan.* Oxford University Press.

Deakin, S and HD Whittaker (2009). Corporate governance, institutions, and the spirit of capitalism Ch, 10. In *Corporate Governance and Managerial Reform in Japan.*

Diamantaras, D (2009). *A Toolbox for Economic Design.* Palgrave McMillan.

Dore, R (1973, 2011). British Factory — Japanese Factory: The Origins of National Diversity in Industrial Relations. Routledge Library Editions, Japan.

Dore, R (2000). Will Global Capitalism be Anglo-Saxon Capitalism [Internet Article: A revised version of a lecture given at the London School of Ecnomics in May 2000].

Doving, E and O Nordhaug (2002). Learning Firm Specific Knowledge and Skills: Conceptual Issues and Empirical Results. Paper presented to OKLC The 3rd European Conference on Organizational Knowledge.

Enright, MJ and V Subramanian (2012). Subsidiary Types, Activities, and Location: An Empirical Investigation. Vierick Leuven Gent Working Paper Series 2012/02.

Fenton-O'Creevy, MP Gooderham and J-L Cerdin (2011). Bridging roles, social skill and embedded knowing in multinational organizations, Ch. 4. In *Politics and Power in Multinational Corporation*.

Foss, NJ (1996). Capabilities and the Theory of the Firm. On-line version from Social Science Research Network.

Fujii, T and K Matsuzaki (2004). Management and Learning in Japanese Corporate Groups (*Japanese*). Dobunkan.

Granovetter, M (1995). Business groups and social organization, Ch. 18. In *The Handbook of Economic Sociology*, Smelser, N and R Swedberg (eds.) Princeton University Press.

Geppert, M and C Dorrenbacher (2011). Politics and power in the multinational corporation: The role of institutions, interests, and identities, Ch. 1, Dörrenbäacher, C and M Geppert (eds.). Cambridge University Press.

Grant, RM (1991). The resource-based theory of competitive advantage: Implications for strategy formulation. *California Management Review*, 33(3), pp. 114–133.

Grossman, S and O Hart (1986). The costs and benefits of ownership: A theory of vertical and lateral integration. *Journal of Political Economy*, 94(4), 691–719.

Hall, PA and D Soskice (2001). *Varieties of capitalism: The institutional foundations of comparative advantage*. Oxford University Press.

Hart, O and J Moore (1990). Property rights and the nature of firms. *Journal of Political Economy*, 98(61), 1119–1157.

Higuchi, J (2002). Re-examination of the Personnel System in Japan (*Japanese*). Hitotsubashi Research Institute (2012). *Industry Map Digest*.

Hosokawa, Hidetoshi (2006). The Role of Information Systems Department: The Environment that CIO Faces. Japan Users Association of Information Systems (Japanese).

Hurwicz, L (1993). Towards a framework for analysing institutions and institutional changes. In *Market and Democracy: Participation, Accountability and Efficiency*, pp. 51–67; Bowles, S, H Gintis and B Gustafsson. Cambridge University Press.

Hvid, M (1999). Long-Term Contracts and Relational Contracts.

Inagami, T and DH Whittaker (2005). The New Community Firm: Employment, Governance and Management Reform in Japan. Cambridge University Press.

Institute for Monetary and Economic Studies (IMES) Bank of Japan (2011). employees benefit and company law: Concerning investment in firm-specific skills. In *Legal Issues Study Group on Corporate Governance (Japanese)*.

Ito, H and T Kikutani and O Hayashida (1997). Hiving-Off Strategy and Power Delegation in Japanese Corporations (*Japanese*). *MITI Research Review*, 10, 24–63.

Ito, H and T Kikutani and O Hayashida (2003). The Multifaceted Relationship between a Company and its Subsidiaries: The Governance of Subsidiaries REITI Discussion Paper Series 03-J-005 (*Japanese*).

Ito, H (2005). Corporate restructuring in Japan: Economic analysis of multi-divisional form organization, Ch. 14. In *Japan's Corporate System*, Vol. 1: *Organization and Coordination*.

Ito, H (2005). Boundary of the firm and economic theories in Japan's corporate system, Ch. 3. Corporation and Governance, Vol. 2.

Ito, H and T Kikutani and O Hayashida (2008). Business portfolio restructuring of Japanese firms in the 1990s: Entry and Exit Analysis, Ch. 8. In *Corporate Governance in Japan — Institutional Change and Organizational Diversity*, Aoki, M, G Jackson and H Miyajima (eds.). Oxford University Press.

Ito, H and Z Shishido (2001). The Firm as a Legal Entity: What Distinguishes Wholly Owned Subsidiaries from Internal Divisions in Japan. www.ssrn.com

Ito, K (1995). Japanese spinoffs: Unexpected survival strategies. *Strategic Management Journal*, 16, 431–446.

Ito, S (2005). Business and organization restructuring based on cost reduction. *Kyoto Management Review* (Japanese), 7.

Iwasaki, N and A Aihara (2005). How to Rebuild the Corporate Design, Economic Studies Seikei University 2005-02, 287–330 (*Japanese*).

Jackson, G and H Miyajima (2008). The diversity and change of corporate governance in Japan, Ch. 1. In *Corporate Governance in Japan — Institutional Change and Organizational Diversity*, Aoki, M, G Jackson and H Miyajima (eds.). Oxford University Press.

Jacoby, SM (2005). *The Embedded Corporation: Corporate Governance and Employment Relations in Japan and the United States*. Princeton University Press.

Japan Association of Corporate Executives (*Keizai Doyukai*) (2009). Creation of New Japanese Style Management. 16th Corporate White Paper. (Japanese).

Japan Small Business Research Institute (2008). M&A in Japan. Research Study on M&A of Medium Small Firms, Ch. 1 (*Japanese*).

Japanese Company Law, Article 2-3 (*Japanese*).

Johnston, S (2005). Headquarters and subsidiaries in multinational corporations: Strategies, tasks and coordination. *Journal of the Institute of Internal Auditors Japan*, No. 6, 2011.

Juntunen, J (2010). Logistics Outsourcing for Economies in Business Networks. University of Oulu G Oeconomica No. 43.

Kali, R (2002). The Nature of the Business Group: Power, Relational Contracts and Scope. www.ssrn.com

Kagotani, M of NTT Data Institute of Management Consulting (2007). In *Search of Current Strategy of IT Subsidiary, Information Future* No. 29 (*Japanese*).

Kaiho, H (1999). On Contributory Role of Overseas Subsidiaries and its Formation: Some Evidence fron an International Comparative Survey (Japanese). Seijo University Economic Paper No. 146, pp. 107–124.

Kato, T and H Owan (2011). Market characteristics, intra-firm coordination, and the choice of human management systems: Theory and evidence. *Journal of Economic Behaviour and Organization*, 80, 375–396.

Komoto, K (2003). Empirical Analysis of Hiving-Off and Corporate Earnings, NLI Research Institute (*Japanese*). Economic Report No. 2002-03, NLI on-line resource.

Kikutani, T and T Saito (2006). Economic Analysis of Wholly Owned Subsidiaries (*Japanese*). Kyoto University Economic Research Working Paper, J53.

Khanna, T and JW Rivkin (2001). Estimating the performance effects of business groups in emerging markets. *Strategic Management Journal.* 22(1), 45–74.

Khanna, T and Y Yafeh (2005). Business groups and risk sharing around the world. *Journal of Business*, 78(1), 301–340.

Kostova, T (1999). Transnational transfer of strategic organizational practices: A contextual perspective. *Academy of Management Review*, 24, 308–324.

Kuritani, H and AT Kearney *et al.* (2010). Reformation of the Functional Subsidiary: Part 1: Making Clear the Management Responsibility of the Parent Company; Part 2: Rectify the Parent Company's Dependence; Part 3: Propose Improvements on Goods and Services, *Nikkan Kogyo* Newspaper, November 3, 10, 17 (*Japanese*).

Langlois, RN and NJ Foss (1997). Capabilities and Governance: The Rebirth of Production in the Theory of Economic Organization. Working Paper No 97-2.

Leff, NH (1978). Industrial organization and entrepreneurship in the developing countries: The economic groups. *Economic Development and Cultural Change*, 26, 661–675.

Lincoln, JR and M Shimotani (2009). Whither the Keiretsu, Japan's Business Networks. Institute for Research on Labor and Employment, Working Paper #188-09.

McFadden, D (2008). The Human Side of Mechanism Design: A Tribute to Leo Hurwicz and Jean-Jacque Laffont. *Review of Economic Design*, 13(1), 77–100.

Ministry of Economy, Trade and Industry (2012). Basic Survey of Corporate Activities (*Japanese — Kigyou Katsudou Kihon Chousa*). MLIT on-line resource.

Ministry of Economy, Trade and Industry (2010). Vision for Industry Structure (*Japanese*). MLIT on-line resource.

Ministry of Economy, Trade and Industry (2007). Medium and Small Size Corporation White Paper, Part 3, Section 3. (*Japanese — Chusho Kigyou Hakusho*). MLIT on-line resource.

Ministry of Finance, Policy Research Institute of the Ministry of Finance (2003). Report of the Research Committee on the Diversity of Japanese Companies and Corporate Governance: Analysis of Business Strategy, Group Management and Decentralized Organizations. Ministry of Finance on-line resource.

Ministry of Health, Labour and Welfare (2012). Annual Skill Development Basic Survey (*Japanese*). MHLW on-line resource.

Ministry of Internal Affairs and Communications (2009). Economy Census — Basic Survey (*Japanese — Keizai Census Kisou Chousa*). MIAC on-line resource.

Ministry of Economy Trade and Industry, Ministry of Health Labour and Welfare, and Ministry of Education Culture Sports Science and Technology (2012). Policies Regarding Enhancement of Core Manufacturing Competencies (*Japanese*).

Miwa, H (2006). Japanese Type of Management Behind Japanese Style of Welfare Nation and its Global Transferability (*Japanese*). *Asia, Japan Journal*, 2007-02, 63–73.

Miyajima, H (2011). How to Understand the Evolution of Japan's Corporate Governance? Towards Redesigning Corporate Governance. RIETI Policy Discussion Paper Series 11-P-009 (*Japanese*).

Miyajima, H (2009). Diversified Evolution of the Japanese Corporate System: Possibility of a Hybrid Model. RIETI Discussion Paper Series 09-J-017 (*Japanese*), 2–48.

Miyajima, H (2009). The Global Financial Crisis and the Evolution of Corporate Governance in Japan.

Miyajima, H (2007). Survey regarding Business Portfolio and Group Formation in Japanese Companies. RIETI Press Release Material.

Miyajima, H (2006). How should we Understand the Surge in M&A? The Historical Development and Economic Role of M&A. RIETI Discussion Paper Series 06-J-044 (*Japanese*).

Miyamoto, D (2006). Relations between Employees Transfers (*Shukko*) and Corporate Performances: An Empirical Analysis for the Japanese Manufacturing Corporate Group. ITEC Working Paper Series 06-09 (*Japanese*).

Mookherjee, D (2005). Decentralization, Hierarchies and Incentives: A Mechanism Design Perspective. *Journal of Economic Literature*, 44(3), 367–390.

Morikawa, M (2012). Structural Transformation of Japanese Companies: Strategy, Internal Organization. Corporate Behaviour RIETI Discussion Paper Series 12-J-017 (*Japanese*).

Motohashi, K (2003). The Japanese model: Shifts in comparative advantage due to the IT revolution and modularization. *Journal of Japanese Trade & Industry*, 30–35.

Nikkei Industry Map (2012). Published by *Nihon Keijai* Newspaper, ISBN 978-4-532-31735-5.

Nonaka, I and H Takeuchi (1995). The Knowledge-Creating Company: How Japanese Companies Create Dynamics of Innovation.

North, DC (1992). Institutions and economic theory. *American Economist*, 3–6.

Okabe, M and S Seki (2006). The Results of Corporate M&A in Japan — Empirical Analysis concerning Management Stability and Efficiency. Policy and Government Research Studies, Working Paper No. 107 (*Japanese*).

Ohara, A (2003). The drastic switch in management system: The case of Matsushita Electric, *The Economic Review of Daichi Keizai Daigaku*, 33(2), 17–37, (*Japanese*).

Olcott, G (2009). Conflict and Change: Foreign Ownership and the Japanese Firm. Cambridge University Press.

O'Reilly, CA and ML Tushman (2004). Ambidextrous organization. *Harvard Business Review*, April.

Order for Enforcement of the Companies Act, Articles 2-1, 2-3, 2-4, 3-3, 8. (*Japanese*). Government on-line resource e-Gov.

Ostrom, E (2011). Background on the institutional analysis and development framework. *The Policy Studies Journal*, 39(1), 7–27.

Otsubo, M (2011). Group Restructuring of Japanese Companies: Change in Ownership Relationship between Parent Company and Listed Subsidiary Company (*Japanese*). Chou Keijai-Sha: Tokyo.

Owan, H (2008, 2009). Organizational and Personnel Economics for MBAs. Keizai (Economics) Seminar No. 636, 1–111.

Prahalad, CK and G Hamel (1990). The core competence of the corporation. *Harvard Business Review*, May–June.

Regulation concerning Consolidated Financial Statements (also Cabinet Ordinance No. 45 of 30th September 2010), Article 4-1-1 (*Japanese*).

Samphantharak, K (2007). The Choice of Organizational Structure: Business Group versus Conglomerate. www.ssrn.com

Schaede, U (2008). Choose and Focus — Japanese Business Strategies for the 21st Century. Cornell University Press.

Securities Listing Regulations, (Yuka Shoken Jyoujyou Kitei) Article 2-1-26 (*Japanese*). Japan Exchange Group on-line resource.

Senda, NH Park and M Hirano (2011). Modularization of work and skill evaluations: Two cases of IT companies. *Japan Labour Review*, 8(3), 6–25.

Shinya, Y (2008). The Effect of Increased System Complexity on Transactions amongst Firms (*Japanese*). Kobe University Current Management Issues, 1–41.

Schmid, S and A Daniel (2011). 'Headquarters-subsidiary relationships from a social psychological perspective: How perception gaps concerning the subsidiary's role may lead to conflict' in politics and power in the multinational corporation, Ch. 8. Dörrenbächer, C and M Geppert. Cambridge University Press.

Schotter, A and PW Beamish (2011). Intra-Organizational Turbulences in Multinational Corporations, Ch. 6. In *Politics and Power in the Multinational Corporation*. Dörrenbächer, C and M Geppert. Cambridge University Press.

Sonoda, T (2004). The applicability of the balanced score card on functional subsidiaries, *Mita Shogaku Kenkyu* 47(1), 211–224. (*Japanese*).

Tanaka, A (2003). Weakening of the six corporate groups (*Japanese*).

Hiki, F, Y Kajusa, N Sawanabe, S Ushio, H Ohata, A Kitai, H Miya, T Tani and N Morita (2010). Amoeba Management — Theory and Practice. Amoeba Management Study Group (Ed.) (*Japanese*).

Teece, DJ (1997). Dynamic capabilities and strategic management. *Strategic Management Journal*, 18(7).

Thelen, K (2004). How Institutions Evolve: The Political Economy of Skills in Germany, Britain, the United States, and Japan. Cambridge University Press.

Tobita, T (2005). Consolidate group management and the creation of corporate value, *Ritsumeikan Management Studies*, 44(2), 83–103.

Tregaskis, O (2003). Learning networks, power and legitimacy in multinational subsidiaries. *The International Journal of Human Resource Management*, 14(3), 431–447.

Van de Ven, AH (2007). Engaged scholarship: A Guide for Organizational and Social Research. Oxford University Press.

Vogel, SK (2006). Japan Remodeled. Cornell University Press.

Watanabe, Yusuke of Funai Soken (2012). Logistics subsidiary pressed for transformation, Monthly Newsletter: *Logistics Inside*, 4, January (Japanese).

Whitley, RG Morgan, W Kelly and D Sharpe (2003). The changing Japanese multinational: Application, adaption and learning in car manufacturing and financial services. *Journal of Management Studies*, 40(3), 644–672.

Williamson, O (1985). The Economic Institutions of Capitalism. The Free Press.

Williamson, O (2002). The Theory of the Firm as Governance Structure: From Choice to Contract. *Journal of Economic Perspectives*, 16(3), 171–195.

Yamaoka, T (2007). Examination concerning organization change and organization models. *Yokohama International Social Science Studies*, 11(4–5).

Yamada, H, M Ando, H Hara and A Tsuji (2009). Changing Towards an Employment System that Fits the Transformation of Industry Structure: Discarding the Disillusion of Life-Time Employment (Japanese). Research Report by the National Institute for Research Advancement (NIRA). Japan.

Yano Research Institute (2007). Survey on Strategy of IT Subsidiaries, Research Express (*Japanese*). Survey Report Summary, Yano Research Institute Online Resource.

Yano Research Institute (2009). Survey on Management of IT Subsidiaries, Research Express (*Japanese*). Survey Report Summary, Yano Research Institute Online Resource.

Yin, RK (2009). Case Study Research: Design and Methods, 4th Edition. SAGE Publications.

INDEX

179

Printed in the United States
By Bookmasters